MW00700792

MIMIKA COONEY

Build Your Author Platform with a Purpose

Marketing Strategies for Writers

First published by Mimika Media 2019

Copyright © 2019 by Mimika Cooney

All rights reserved. No part of this publication may be reproduced, stored or transmitted in any form or by any means, electronic, mechanical, photocopying, recording, scanning, or otherwise without written permission from the publisher. It is illegal to copy this book, post it to a website, or distribute it by any other means without permission.

Mimika Cooney asserts the moral right to be identified as the author of this work.

Mimika Cooney has no responsibility for the persistence or accuracy of URLs for external or third-party Internet Websites referred to in this publication and does not guarantee that any content on such Websites is, or will remain, accurate or appropriate.

Designations used by companies to distinguish their products are often claimed as trademarks. All brand names and product names used in this book and on its cover are trade names, service marks, trademarks and registered trademarks of their respective owners. The publishers and the book are not associated with any product or vendor mentioned in this book. None of the companies referenced within the book have endorsed the book.

First edition

ISBN: 978-1-7322848-6-9

Editing by Mich Nicholas

This book was professionally typeset on Reedsy.
Find out more at reedsy.com

Contents

Invitation   v
Foreword   vii

I   Platform Building

Introduction   3
Why Build a Platform?   4
What Is a Platform?   10
Avoid Wasting Time, Money & Effort   14
Establishing Authority as an Influencer   26
Analogue Days   31
What Publishers & Readers Want   35
Write the Right Book   40

II   Branding Blueprint

Branding Blueprint   47
Understanding Your Marketing Strategy   61
Personalized Website   65

III   Email Marketing

Build an Email List of Raving Fans   79
Create a Freebie Offer That Hooks Readers Fast   84
Landing Pages   88
Email Funnels that Sell while you Sleep   91
How to Setup a CRM   94

IV   Social Media & Promotions

Promotional Ideas   101
The Power of Video   113
Paid Advertising   120
Extra Offers   123
About the Author   125
References   127
Notes   131

Invitation

As a thank you for purchasing this book, I would love to gift you with the printable version of the accompanying **Platform Building Checklist**. Print out this tool to help you work through the book as you follow along. Download here **www.mimikacooney.com/platform**

BUILD YOUR
**AUTHOR
PLATFORM**
WITH A PURPOSE
IN 30 DAYS

FREE CHECKLIST
WWW.MIMIKACOONEY.COM/PLATFORM

Foreword

This book will change your life! Build Your Author Platform with a Purpose is one of the best books on the subject I have read in a long time. Mimika has pulled together a concise guide to discover your audience and develop a modern 21st century Internet marketing plan. You would pay thousands of dollars on training courses and coaching to get this information. I appreciate her practical step-by-step approach including check lists and resources.

Doug Addison

Author of 'Hearing God Everyday' & Best known for the Daily Prophetic Words & Spirit Connection Podcast & Blog

A solid introduction to platform building for authors.

Alinka Rutkowska

USA Today Best-Selling Author & CEO of Leaders Press

Rarely do I engage with a platform building training and agree wholeheartedly with it. This book is the exception. If you are new to the idea of platform building, or are in the middle of it with some unanswered questions, this is a very useful resource. Mimika Cooney delivers on everything listed in the book's description. You will avoid a lot of mistakes and find the platform growing process accelerated by doing what she spells out in this much-needed book.

Anna LeBaron

Social Media & Book Launch Expert & Author of 'The Polygamist's Daughter: A Memoir'

I

Platform Building

1

Introduction

For years I was being selfish. There was something I needed to say, and I just couldn't spit it out. It took me years to realize this clandestine concept. There are people who are waiting, praying, wishing, longing, hoping, stressing over, and dreaming about a resolution that only *I* could provide.

Let me introduce you to a realization. You were born to share your story, your talents, your gifts and your message of hope—for someone for such a time as this! So what is holding you back? For many, it's fear. Fear of the unknown, fear of failure, fear of disappointment, or fear of success.

Can you imagine what your life would look like on the other side of fear? Can you imagine that feeling of accomplishment when you have completed that *thing* that you know you were meant to do? You know, that burning internal desire, that perpetual idea that can't let you go. *That* thing.

It's supposed to be you. No one else has the skills, abilities, backstory, failures, triumphs, mechanics, or DNA like you. Didn't think you were *that* important, right?

If you have been given something of value, it's not for you to keep. It's for others. So don't you think that you are being selfish if you don't share it with others? God gave you whatever the *thing* is to give away, and if you're not putting yourself out there, isn't that more selfish?

So what are you waiting for?

2

Why Build a Platform?

As a writer and podcaster, I'm fascinated by stories. As a little girl, I loved reading the Enid Blyton *Faraway Tree* book series. My mother bought a "state-of-the-art" typewriter when I was 10, and I thought myself so fancy typing up stories that would pop into my head. Even mistakes were exciting because I had good old Tippex (or white out) I could paint over the erroneous words.

Fast forward a few decades and I've learnt a thing or two about writing, marketing, and sharing a message. As a TV host, professional photographer, podcaster, writer, and marketer with 25 years' experience, I've had to learn some hard lessons by making many, many mistakes. What I'm sharing with you today I have learnt in the trenches attending the school of knocks.

When I had the opportunity to publish my very first book, I was ecstatic! My dream of being a published author was finally going to be a reality. However, my biggest disappointment was realizing that the publisher was not going to do the promotional work for me. If you are a huge celebrity, you will probably have agents scurrying around you to help. But let's face it, most of us are not celebs but average Joes with big dreams.

If you want to be successful, you have to take the reins and do the work yourself. This is especially true when you are just starting out. It can seem unfair that when you need the help the most, help is scarce. But I know that you're a smart cookie because you are reading this book!

In a recent training, I asked my students what their single biggest challenge was with building a platform. The answers included:

"Finding it hard to determine who my audience is and what I want to offer";

"How to find the right audience whom I'm meant to serve";

"Winning the trust of the right people in getting their attention;,

"Understanding technology because I'm illiterate";

"Not knowing where to start because I feel completely overwhelmed."

If you can relate, then you are definitely not alone. These are very common responses that I've heard because many of us, including myself, started the exact same way. If you've been concerned that you can't succeed, or if you failed at this in the past, I want you to know that it's not your fault. I want to put those fears to rest because I know that you can do it; you just need the right person to explain it to you.

There is a lot of information that can be so confusing and sometimes counter intuitive. One person will say one thing, somebody else will say another. Information overload can keep you from actually getting success and taking action. It's the whole paralysis by analysis syndrome. So my goal is to be able to guide you through this marketing process and make it a whole lot easier for you (especially if marketing is not your jam).

Many people think that you have to be a celebrity or a big name to have influence. That only big companies can afford to build a platform, or do marketing, or create advertising campaigns. Or perhaps that you need a lot of money or a fancy college degree to be successful. I'm here to tell you those are all false! They're all complete myths. Contrary to what you've seen or heard before, there are pretty much no more barriers to entry anymore. Perhaps 15 or 20 years ago traditional marketing worked that way, but that was before the days of the Internet. Now we know that the Internet has interrupted society and totally changed the way we do things. The likes of social media have given us the opportunity to be directly in front of the ideal people we are trying to reach.

So what is the big dream? I'm sure you have a dream to change the world and make a big impact, because that is what you want influence for, right? The difference is that I actually care about your success. I truly want to see you living the life of your dreams because I have spent so many years feeling frustrated. I know how hard disappointment can be.

I am a strong believer in the call of God to step up and walk out my divine purpose and life calling. I've always felt this clarion call, wanting to understand my purpose, and to show up in the world using my gifts for the benefit of others. This is why I love to write books for the Christian Living non-fiction genre offering life lessons through my own mistakes.

The Parable of the Talents is a great example. The master goes away and leaves his servants with different amounts of talents, which is very indicative of what we're all about today. We all have different talents, we all have different skills, but it's how we use them and how we serve others that determine our success. As the story goes, he rewards the servant who was able to multiply his talents and use them for the greater good. What did he say to the servant who buried his talents in the sand? He called him wicked, evil, and lazy.

I can guess that if you're reading this book, you definitely don't want to be in that category. I can guess that you want to use your gifts and talents to walk out your purpose, because there are things that only *you* can do and the world is waiting for them.

Here is another encouragement. I want you to know that your message matters. Here are some reviews for my two books that I had published. These reviews that you can see for yourself are on Amazon for the book (a) *Mindset Make Over: How to Renew your Mind and Walk in God's Authority*

"Mimika has written a wonderfully thought-provoking book in Mindset Make Over. It gets to the heart of stinking thinking. She helps the reader focus on gaining a more intimate relationship with God."

"This is the latest book I've started reading. I've been up at until 2:30 AM I must say, it's definitely started a healing process. I was too ashamed to admit I needed, it's a mastery."

Here is somebody who doesn't know me personally, who found my book on Amazon. It's my no-holds-barred life story of a really hard journey I had to walk through personally. Even though it was a really hard process writing and birthing this book, I'm so excited and honored that my story is helping others.

You don't know how someone needs to hear what you've been through, and how you've been able to overcome things. Your story will empower others to walk through whatever they're going through right now.

I want to encourage you to be confident in the fact that what you have to say is really important. You'll know something you really *have* to do because the desire never goes away. You will see confirmation in different ways. Either someone will say something to you that perks up your ears, or you'll see a movie, or hear music, or read a book. These are all road signs. You will eventually recognize the nudges and start to get the picture when you see it repeated over and over. It's the *thing* that you're called to do.

Here is a comment I received on social media saying;

"I don't need to put any effort into building my platform because if God wants my ministry to grow, He will bring the people to me."

Newsflash...sorry, honey, but I don't agree with that. You have to show up and put yourself in front of the right people for them to find you. It doesn't matter whether you're in business or in ministry, you need to be visible where your people are gathering. Whether they're reading books or watching movies or YouTube, you need to show up in the right places and be present. You need to put the effort into being discoverable.

Having volunteered for a year at Elevation Church in the video production department, I realized that there are people in far-off places like Bangladesh and Singapore and the darkest parts of Africa, who are starving for connection and community. Anyone can show up and share their skills using modern technology. So there is no excuse for you not to be able to use what is out there!

I really do feel there is an urgency for thought leaders to step up and be the light that the world needs. Just look at the media lately—what a hot mess! We need to infiltrate the media with good news. We need to turn the tides on all the negativity, and the only way we can do that is by answering the call to join the army of light workers.

It can feel very hard standing on a soapbox yelling when no one wants to listen. Right? That is the whole point. If you build a platform right, you won't have to yell because it is not about you. If you realize that what you have to share is not about you, it takes the pressure off. It's about being used as a tool; you just need to get out of your own way. Walking in your purpose and doing what you feel you are called to do is important.

My goals for you in reading this book is that I want you to walk away feeling confident that you can do this marketing thing. I want you to achieve your dreams and goals as quickly as possible. I know from personal experience that I've spent years either delaying things or sabotaging myself because of fear. Regret from missed opportunities. I was either too scared or didn't know how to do it.

I want you to have the tools that you need to easily implement, without having to spend thousands of dollars on expensive coaches, courses, and consultants. I say this because I am an expensive consultant! I've worked with several clients managing their marketing. I've used the same strategies to implement in their businesses and brands that I'm going to share with you.

By being a respected influencer in your niche, you can make a greater impact when somebody values your voice. And that is exactly what a platform is. Giving your voice a microphone. It's about elevating your voice above the noise.

I want to guide you towards success using a step-by-step strategy. By continuing to throw spaghetti at the wall hoping it will stick is not a strategy. I don't want you to waste any more time and money on expensive mistakes. I also don't want the world to miss out on your own unique gifts and talents.

You're going to learn incremental steps and you will get better as you go along. So don't beat yourself up if you're not where you want to be, but thank goodness you're not where you used to be! Right?

Technology changes constantly, and it can be hard and confusing to keep up. I love reading books and I love to keep up-to-date with what is going on in the marketing and business world. I love to learn and then teach what I've learned. Over the years, I developed a system and repeatable strategy that I applied to my different businesses and different markets, and realized there is a foundation that you can build that leads you to the path of success.

I really believe in creating something once right from the beginning, instead of wasting effort fixing a bad job later. Once you have figured out the process, you can just rinse and repeat and apply it over again. Every time you launch a book or a new product or start a new business, you can use the same system. Obviously, things do change, but if you've got the elements of a great foundation, you can follow that wherever you are.

This book is designed for you especially if you have a valuable message to share and only you can share it. If you want to take control of how you show up and are heard online, if you're an entrepreneur who wants a way to attract customers, if you're an author who wants to publish a book, if you're a speaker who wants to establish yourself as an authority, if you're a minister who needs a way to reach and serve your congregation, buckle your seatbelt this is going to be a fun ride!

3

What Is a Platform?

Recently, I conducted a survey of my audience and I wanted to know what their single biggest struggle was with getting their message out into the world. They said their biggest challenge was building a platform so others would listen. Some answers included:

"I don't even know where to start."

"How do I get the word out?"

"I start off gangbusters and lose momentum and become inconsistent."

"Finding time and knowing where to start."

Perhaps this is you? You have grandiose ideas of changing the world. You want to write a book, start a business, or launch a ministry. You've got an idea in your heart, you want to get it out there, but it can be hard juggling so many plates. You want to be known for something and for your contribution to the world. You want to create content so people will listen to your message, because it will change lives.

Perhaps one of the biggest obstacles holding you back is that you feel that marketing, promotion and sales feel icky to you? Maybe you come from the old school of thought that it is up to others to talk about you and spread your message? Or perhaps you're an introvert and the thought of putting yourself "out there" seems braggy, self-indulgent and egotistical?

Let me share what Jerry B. Jenkins says about why you need a platform. Jerry is the bestselling author of the *Left Behind* book series (along with co-author

Tim LaHaye) that sold close to 80 million copies, and author of 150 other successful books. Jerry said he didn't become a full-time freelance writer until his 90th published book, and his bestseller *Left Behind* was his 125th book.

"Publishers don't get excited about invisible authors. You could write an excellent book, but without a national platform, name recognition, and credibility, you'll find it nearly impossible to persuade a publisher to gamble on it. If the idea of building a media platform scares you because you're an introvert and just want to be left alone to write: 1—Get over it, because you can let your alter ego play that part and retreat to your comfort zone later, like I do. 2—If you don't build a platform, you will not get published. Sorry." - (b) Jerry Jenkins

The simple truth is without a platform, nobody will know about you. It doesn't matter if you've written the most life-changing book, or created the most outstanding product, or have an intense passion to help people. If people don't know about you, does it even exist?

It's important to remember that in writing, in building a business, and in life, there are no shortcuts to success. It's about forging ahead the hard way, through trial and error, testing what works and what doesn't. Learning from failures when they are seen as experiments, and building one brick at a time.

What Exactly Is a Platform?

According to dictionary.com the term (c) "Platform" means:

- a horizontal surface or structure with a horizontal surface raised above the level of the surrounding area.
- a raised flooring or other horizontal surface, such as in a hall or meeting place, a stage for use by public speakers, performers, etc.
- the raised area between or alongside the tracks of a railroad station, from which the cars of the train are entered.
- the open entrance area, or the vestibule, at the end of a railroad passenger car.
- a landing in a flight of stairs.

- a public statement of the principles, objectives, and policy of a political party, especially as put forth by the representatives of the party in a convention to nominate candidates for an election.

It reminds me of those old black and white movies from the 1940s where the little boy standing on a tomato box yells, "Extra! Extra! Read all about it!" while trying to sell newspapers for a penny.

In today's society, the term *platform* simply means how you stand out in a crowded marketplace. If you don't elevate your voice on a "platform" you simply blend into the crowd. Whether you want to stand on a stage, or you want to be a full-time author, or change culture with your idea, in order for you to spread that message, you need a platform.

For authors, having a platform means you have a method for readers to find you and hear about your work. If you're in business, then let me tell you that writing a book is the best business card you can have!

Building a platform in the 21st century can feel like an insurmountable task, especially if the idea of marketing scares you. If someone doesn't actually help you through the process and show you the steps you need to take, it can seem almost impossible. The good news is that it does not have to be hard!

Think about this...how would you feel if you were seen as an influencer and your message spread throughout the world? Being an influencer means that your ideas and what you believe are given a voice and amplification. People will stop to take notes and listen to what you have to say. How would that change your life? How would you feel if this was something that people valued, and look to you for advice and assurance?

This book is designed to make it easy for you to build your platform, especially if:

- You're a thought leader who is building a platform for influence.
- You're a writer with a dream of publishing a book, and you know you need to build a platform to get a publisher's attention.
- You've written a book and you don't know what to do next to get the word

out because you are a writer and you don't know a thing about marketing.

- You're a mission-driven entrepreneur with a big dream to create services or products that will transform lives or change culture.
- You want to become a paid speaker, but you don't have an audience yet.
- You want to build your authority in a niche so you can teach, speak, or minister.

In this book, we are going to go through actionable and easy-to-follow tips that you can implement, especially if marketing is not your jam or you're an introvert (who prefers to hide in your writing closet).

We are going to cover these important topics:

- The common marketing mistakes you must avoid that will save you time, money, and loads of effort.
- How to establish yourself as an Authority.
- How to create a Freebie that hooks readers fast.
- How to build an Email List of raving fans.
- How to set up an Email Funnel that works while you sleep.

If this sounds a little too techie, don't worry. I'm going to take you through establishing a solid foundation for your platform, step-by-step, so you can simply rinse and repeat. Think of me like your business and book baby doula: I'm here to help you birth ideas, a book, a business, or a ministry!

Note: The strategies I will be sharing are based on my personal experiences. Please don't feel overwhelmed that you have to do everything all at once. Start with one thing, implement and test results.

4

Avoid Wasting Time, Money & Effort

The Clarion Call

For years, I felt drawn to speak, to write, and to share my story. I had this idea of writing a book for years. My kids would roll their eyes at me when I mentioned it because I kept talking about it, but never did anything about it. I had this burning desire to share my life story in a book or make a movie because my life has been filled with enough drama and moments that it would be a blockbuster! So after spending years toying with the idea, I finally decided to do something about it.

For my birthday, I chose to buy a ticket to the She Speaks Conference run by Proverbs 31 Ministries. It's a three-day conference for aspiring speakers and authors, and offers workshops and training for inspiration and support. I vividly remember going to the conference feeling full of hope. Watching the speakers on stage got me thinking, "I really want to be the one on stage sharing my story. I know I can share stories that way reaching people with a message of hope." I heard the words in my spirit, "So what are you waiting for? I've given you everything you need. You just need to make a decision to do it." I was like, "Yikes! Okay, let's do this!"

They offered appointments with publishers and agents. If you wanted to pitch your idea in the hope of getting publishing appointments, you had to put together a book proposal and a one sheet. It basically describes who you are, what you want to write about, a pitch for your book idea and your marketing plan. I really wanted to pitch my idea to a particular agent, but I didn't know whom I would be pitching to until the last minute because I was on the waitlist. I had seven days to put together a book proposal which is a crazy short amount of time.

With my two appointments, I pitched the idea of writing a memoir. The first time I met with an agent, she bluntly said, "Memoirs don't sell," and passed on my idea immediately. I was devastated. What I heard was *"your story doesn't matter, no one cares about what you have to say."* I had these high hopes and they got dashed, and it was very disheartening. How else was I going to make this work?

What I didn't know was that a lot of the time, publishers attend conferences knowing exactly what they're looking for. They already know the kind of books they want to publish because they have experience with a particular genre or category. You can get rejected simply because you're just not the right fit for that publisher (irrespective of whether your writing is good or not). With any kind of creativity or art, you have to be ready to be rejected *a lot*. Sometimes, it's just about timing and being able to fit the brief; other times, it is about finding a gap in the market and filling it. It starts with a great idea, a hungry market, and someone who knows how to position the idea correctly. It's about market fit which is uber important in any business.

After getting over the disappointment, I realized that she was right. Unless you are a big name, like the Chip and Joanna Gaines of the world, nobody really cares. I had to be brutally honest with myself: no one cares to know about my memoir because they don't know who I am. But I'm a tough cookie and I don't take no for an answer. Since I got rejected in one way, I was determined to find another way to make it work. So I started investigating the avenue of self-publishing and I realized: "Wow, light bulb moment. I don't have to wait for permission. I don't have to ask people's permission to actually do this. I know what I'm called to do and I'm going to figure out how to make it happen!"

I took the feedback I received and then wrote a non-fiction book which became *Worrier to Warrior: A Mother's Journey from Fear to Faith.* It was my story of walking through the journey of depression and anxiety, dealing with a child with learning issues and suicidal thoughts, overcoming grief, and how I was able to show the hope of God's message through my experiences. However, I packaged it and framed it as a non-fiction book in the Women's Christian Living category, and it sold well and continues to sell today!

The good news is that your story can still be told, but in another way if you position and package it correctly.

The Wake-up Call

When you buy a book, you're buying a book for *you* as the reader. You are asking yourself "What is in it for me? What am I going to learn from this book? What can this author help me with in my life right now?"

I'm particularly referring to non-fiction books, but it is the same concept for fiction writers and for business owners. Often we can lose sight of the big picture, which is that you are writing books and creating products to *serve* people. If you're interested in creating a platform to serve others, you really have to consider what your audience wants, and not what you want to share. Using your story as a way of framing the lesson makes it so much easier to absorb. It's called the "come alongside me" approach.

For Christian writers, many of us go through the process of wrestling with God about sharing our story. Once we decide to share it, we think everyone is going to love the idea just because we think it's important. You need to know that the message is important because it's *not* about you. It's about what God wants to do in you and through you that really counts. Someone out there is in pain, crying, pleading, and praying for an answer to their prayers. Your book and your message are the hope they need to pull themselves out of despair to give them the hope that points them towards life.

Perhaps you put something out into the world and it gets rejected, and your hope is dashed. But sometimes it's not that the idea was bad. It wasn't positioned correctly and it was not presented to the right audience. I would advise that you have somebody else have eyes on your work. You need someone like a coach, editor, or business partner who can support you and give you some hard truths to help you avoid costly mistakes. You need honest feedback like "I know you like this idea, but this isn't what is going to sell." You will have to develop thick skin because at times, it is going to hurt.

I believe books are an awesome platform built for longevity that are easily shared. They will carry spreading your message long after you are gone. If you are willing and open and prepared to put your fears aside, you can do amazing things. Remember, it's about the person on the other side who is going to read your book and how important it will be in changing their life. Think of it this way: the longer you sit on it, you are delaying somebody else's breakthrough!

You already have the vision, and sometimes, you need to step out, even though you might be scared or you're not sure what to expect. You start by inching forward, and then you can course correct. If you sit there staying stuck, you're never going to go anywhere. I can guarantee that you will get rejected at times, but if you persist, you will get noticed. Are you willing to take that first step?

15 Common Mistakes Authors Make

Mistake #1 - Not Having a Plan or Strategy

Throwing a book out there and just hoping that Amazon will sell it for you is called hope marketing. It simply doesn't work like that. It's very important to have a strategy. I don't know about you, but I love lists. I have to have a list that I can tick off so I feel like I've actually achieved something. It gives me a way of staying focused. I can suffer from distraction very easily and go down these little rabbit holes with every little shiny thing that comes along. This is why it's important to have a branding strategy or blueprint, an understanding of who I am and whom I serve. When you have opportunities come across your path, you can easily say no or yes because you know if it fits within your blueprint and plan.

Start with the end in mind. Where do you want to end up with your goal? Is it to become a paid speaker, launch a product or program, or become a full-time author? Writing a book is an awesome way to start because it is the best business card. If you want to write a series of books, think about the series and work your way back.

Keeping up with social media can be a total time suck. That is why strategy and planning are so important. Knowing what you want to achieve is crucial as every platform functions differently. The way you treat Instagram is different from the way you use Facebook, but again, it first depends on discovering where your ideal audience is.

Mistake #2 - Writing the Wrong Book

Writing the wrong book will cost you time, money, and loads of frustration. Many writers get disappointed when their book doesn't sell well because it doesn't resonate with an audience. For instance, I had this whole plan for writing a memoir and plan for the chronological order of what I wanted to say, but I realized it was the wrong book! Even though it was painful to hear, it saved me six months of hard work writing a book that no one would want to read. That is why it's so important to do ample research for the categories, audience, keywords, and positioning *before* writing a single word. This is exactly what a publisher would do to find the perfect market fit for a book idea.

Mistake #3 - Writing for Yourself and Not the Audience

Many creators and artists make the mistake of writing a book or creating a product for themselves and not an audience. When you are starting out, you want to share your story with the world. You want to write from your perspective because you feel justified by what you've experienced. However, if it's not for the right audience or how *they* see things, your writing is going to fall on deaf ears. Consider who that person is. Who is sitting on the other end of the table? Who is the reader, or the listener, or the audience? Where is she in her life and what is she doing? What is she thinking about, and how can you help her?

Mistake #4 - Ignoring the Need to Build a Platform

In marketing and publishing, we talk about platform. It's when someone has a voice, has something to say, and uses methods to share their message with a wider audience. Whether it's speaking on stage, making videos, writing books, or creating products, you need a platform if you want your message to spread far and wide. A platform is built mostly online these days through TV, YouTube, radio, websites, blogs, magazines, or social media.

A platform helps you to be seen and heard above the crowd. If you want to be someone of influence that others notice, you need to get over yourself. You need a platform. It's not about putting your art out there hoping that if you build it, they will come. Sorry to disappoint you but that simply doesn't work anymore. Times have changed and technology has changed the competitive landscape. If you're serious about your message, then you need to take building your platform seriously as one of your main priorities. Think of it this way: you have something valuable to teach but you're teaching to an empty classroom. We need to get those bums on seats!

Mistake #5 - Not Treating a Platform Like a Business

Not treating platform-building like a business is like throwing spaghetti against the wall hoping it will stick. Trying random tactics or marketing methods based on what everyone else is doing is often not very effective, and utterly exhausting. You need to think about your efforts just like someone running a business. Where is your audience and what daily tasks can I do to put myself in front of them? When you think of it as a business, you will be consistent with your efforts and measure your results.

Mistake #6 - Copying Other People's Ideas and Getting Frustrated When It Doesn't Work

Using someone else's process can be a waste of time especially when the important middle steps are skipped. What you see online can be deceiving. You might hear someone say, "Just do this and you'll get this immediate result and make millions of dollars!" That is just not true. It may look like plain sailing, but underneath they are flapping furiously like a duck on water in a storm. There are a lot of important steps that you might be missing out on. You don't have to do it the same way as everyone else, but you can shortcut your efforts when you make decisions based on what will work for you.

Mistake #7 - Ignoring the Importance of a Professionally Designed Cover

People do judge a book by its cover. It's a simple fact. How are they going to read what you have written if the cover is not enticing? Think about how they promote movies. You will notice that the covers and movie posters that sell well are clean, bright, and the messaging is clear and precise. Often, professional photography is used with either the author, actors, or models to tell a story with crisp quality. I see this so many times with newbie authors and it hurts my eyeballs. When you go cheap designing a cover by doing it yourself (when you're not a designer), it looks cheap and negatively affects the perceived value of the content. Or they pick a cover with a photo or artwork because it's sentimental or meaningful to them personally, but has no connection on what the book is about. Most writers are not designers and have no clue what good design looks like. I like to think of my book cover just like a movie poster with all the right cues and feels.

Admittedly, I personally have designed some of my own book covers and taken the photos myself. This is only because I've been a professional photographer and graphic designer for 15 years. However, I still get feedback from other designers and my audience to make sure my book covers are resonating and telling the right story. I do a ton of research within the category to assess if my design idea aligns with the content. I have the personal belief that if I'm going to do something, I'm going to do it well. Why would I cheapen the importance of my work by slapping together poorly designed packaging? It's important to put in the effort to ensure you are making a good first impression.

No matter whether you are self-publishing or working through a publisher, the cover needs to look professional. If you are not a graphic designer make sure to hire someone who is. You can find very talented designers and professional photographers at affordable prices on places like (d) Reedsy, (e) Fiverr, (f) 99designs or (g) Upwork. You can also buy ready-made covers online through Creative Market or Etsy.

Mistake #8 - Not Hiring a Professional Editor and Proofreader

When starting out, it can be tempting to omit paying for an editor or proofreader, especially when you're on a tight budget. However, bad grammar and typos will soon be apparent in the bad reviews you receive. With the first run of my book, I had read it, re-read it, and had 10 friends and family proofread it. I was horrified to discover that there were still errors after it went to print! The good thing about self-publishing is that I could quickly correct the mistakes without having to fork out on a huge print run. Hiring an editor may seem expensive, but it will save you time and be one of the best investments you can make.

Mistake #9 - Expecting that the Publisher Will Do All the Marketing

The traditional publishing industry is a business and their goal is to make money from publishing books. They have a very narrow focus of who they like to publish based on past performance. They have limited resources and they will prefer to hedge their bets on an author with a proven track record. Unless you're a big name, publishers don't want to do the hard work of promotion unless they have a guarantee of success. They'll add fuel to the fire, but they expect you to start the spark. Many bestselling authors you see that are backed by a big publisher have a large following and they are guaranteed to sell their books. You can have a stake in the ground by showing publishers that you've got what it takes by building your assets and platform right now. This will help you better position yourself to have your book acquisitioned in the future.

Mistake #10 - Giving Up before Starting

No one becomes an overnight success; that's not real life. Think about how many authors, singers, restaurants, and entrepreneurs are in the world. Just because there is competition doesn't mean you should give up or not even try. Competition is fierce, but don't let that deter you. Everybody has an idea and everyone thinks their idea is original. In an echo chamber your idea might seem original to you, but it might not actually *be* an original. Even if it's been done before, it doesn't mean that you can't do it, too. How many Italian restaurants are there? How many pizza places are there? They all do it in different ways. Competition is a good thing—it means that there is a market for your idea. Don't discount yourself because you're not some big name yet.

Mistake #11 - Not Focusing on the Importance of Building an Email List

Building an email list is very important especially when you consider that we don't own our social media platforms. In 2019 both Facebook and Instagram went down and caused a major uproar when they were inaccessible. Think of it this way: Mr. Zuckerberg is your landlord and he rents you space on Facebook. At anytime he can shut it down, kick you out, and you'll lose access to all the contacts you've built up over time. The only way you can avoid catastrophe is to curate your own contacts by building your own email list. Once you have someone's email, you get direct contact with them. Not building an email list soon enough in the promotional process is one way to delay results.

Mistake #12 - Putting All Your Eggs in the Social Media Basket

If you don't have a website and you're not collecting email addresses, you are relying on other platforms to promote yourself and get yourself out there. That is a very slippery slope because remember, Mr. Zuckerberg is your landlord. He dictates access and price, and he can make algorithm changes. He can change the agreements anytime to the way we use the platform. Even though it's free to have a social media page or account, as a business who wants to reach a targeted audience, paying for advertising will provide great results.

Mistake #13 - Confusing Amazon with a Bookstore

There are many book distributors online but the majority of the market buys books from Amazon. It has a very large reach especially here in the USA. What we may overlook about Amazon is that it's a search engine, not a bookstore. Publishing a book and hoping that somebody will discover it is a rookie mistake. Think about when you search for something on Google or YouTube or Amazon, you type in keywords or phrases. Amazon behaves like a search engine and is organized through an algorithm. It's designed to categorize and organize its products to give the user the best possible match. When you have used keywords, categories, and a well-written book description, the algorithm recognizes that your book is valuable and shows it to more people.

Mistake #14 - Not Sharing about Your Book Project Early Enough

If you are thinking about writing a book, post on social media, show a picture of you at the coffee shop typing. The solution to getting unstuck is involving your friends, family, and community right from the start. It builds connection and community over a shared goal. If you are trying to find motivation to get over writer's block, share the process. People love being behind the scenes. It's why things like *America's Got Talent* and *American Idol* did so well as we love watching the process; it's so addictive.

Don't be afraid to ask for feedback. Accepting criticism along the way is important when you involve people early. If you have a few ideas of what you want to write about, you can ask your audience and friends to help you decide so you write the right book. Based on the feedback I received from people with my first book, I changed the title and adjusted some of the content to ensure it fit the right audience. Being willing to course correct is super important and will save you a lot of effort in the future.

Mistake #15 - Not Creating Automated Solutions that Work while You Sleep

If you're on the hamster wheel constantly creating content, you will burn out. Trying to keep up by posting online 12 times a day is not sustainable. Granted, you have to stay current by keeping your audience up-to-date. However, there are systems that you can use to automate some of the repeatable tasks so you can find the time to do other things. What I like to do with my clients is set up a funnel framework. These systems are designed to work while you sleep like sending automated emails when people join your email list. While you focus on filling the top of your funnel, creating new content and engaging with your audience, it keeps working for you consistently. That is how you get brand recognition. By consistently showing up and being associated with the kind of content you stand for. If your audience keeps seeing your name posting valuable content, you're staying front of mind.

Mistake #16 - Not Measuring Results

You need to follow steps and implement each of the steps, then measure every part of the process and tweak as you go along. Even though you might start with an idea, where you end up with may differ if you're not measuring results. You can change a strategy based on your results, whether good or bad. Is posting in a Facebook group getting new readers? Is running a paid Amazon ad selling books? How will you know what to focus on if you're trying too many things without a way of knowing what is working? If you don't have a way of measuring your results, you'll spin your wheels and waste your resources.

A simple gauge of audience growth is how much your email list is growing. If your efforts are not consistently building your email database of fans and followers, all your efforts online will be hard to track.

5

Establishing Authority as an Influencer

I n today's age, we are so enamored with celebrity. It's like if you don't have thousands and thousands of people following you, you feel like you can't reach anybody. Obviously that works for advertisers. They want as many eyeballs as possible. But as an individual, as an entrepreneur, as a coach, as a speaker, as a solopreneur, you're providing a product and a service to people. What you need to know is that you don't need a huge email list to start. You don't need a ton of fans and you don't need to be some celebrity to be an influencer. You just need a very targeted, very specific niche, a list of people that you serve.

The thing is, an influencer literally means that you are influencing people for good or bad. Whether it's improving their life, offering a product, or providing a service. You are helping people find a solution to their problem. You just need to reach those who want to hear from you. It's learning to speak your ideal audience language. Becoming an influencer through experience or knowledge is how you establish that authority. It means that people value what you have to say. You are able to provide them with tools so that they come back to you and listen for more. It doesn't have to be complicated.

As you start putting out content, and as you start to give out more and more value, you are creating brand equity. As your email list grows, your authority grows. As your authority grows, the more things you can offer. Eventually, over time, you can increase the value of what you offer.

26

It's about finding resonance with a market and providing more of what they want. It's what big companies do with intention, test and tweak before investing a ton of cash into an idea that might flop. Try something, test it and tweak it, and if it doesn't work, try it again. Once you've established yourself as an authority, you can charge more money. And that's why it's important to have that brand recognition.

The Business of Branding

I often wondered why companies would spend so much money on placing billboards on the side of the highway where you see it for a flash of a second. I've come to realize that it's a reminder, it's awareness, it's name recognition. It's called branding.

Branding is important. Everybody thinks of the swish when they think of Nike, just like you think of red and white when you think of Coca-Cola. Branding is knowing what to expect from a brand and it makes it comfortable for the consumer. Branding is not reserved only for big companies, though. Branding is how people *feel* about you.

With marketing, it takes 7 to 10 touches before a consumer makes a purchasing decision. It's when people see you on Facebook, then Instagram, then Pinterest, then someone talks about you, then they see you mentioned on somebody's Facebook feed. Until one day they ask, *"Why do I keep hearing about this person?"* Branding helps people to know, like, and trust you.

The thing about branding is, it helps to keep things clear because a confused mind always says no. Instead of taking the time to figure out the confusion, people will just say no and walk away. It happens when there are too many options and it feels overwhelming to make a decision. It's too much for the brain to process so it would rather shut off.

In today's super saturated world, you have to make a lot more noise to be heard. It doesn't have to be obnoxious noise, but it has to be consistent and at the right pitch. Just like a dog whistle, branding can serve the purpose of making your ideal audience's ears perk up and listen.

Branding creates an emotional connection. Having an emotional connection with your audience will increase your potential for higher investment. If they feel comfortable and they know, like, and trust you, they've made that emotional connection with you. When you trust a brand, you are more likely to invest more money and become a repeat buyer.

TV shows and movies build on a brand story. If you've ever binged on a TV series you love, you might not have noticed why you got hooked. Often it is because the characters create an emotional connection with you, and you relate to their plight or challenge.

The same thing applies when you're writing a book. There is a story that you recognize in your own life and it makes you feel comfortable. Your ideal target audience determines your brand style. So for example, if you're writing a book for women that are high powered execs and are climbing the corporate ladder, they perhaps will have a different style to a stay-at-home mom. Neither is good or bad: it just depends on who *you* are talking to. It's like speaking two different languages. You really need to get into the mind of who you are writing your book for, and build your brand voice and style around your audience.

We are living in an era of specificity. In other words, you've got to specify and speak directly to your intended audience. The broad brush treatment doesn't work anymore. We need to be able to speak to them in their language and narrow it down.

Positioning - The Joshua Bell Experiment

This is a real story. Joshua Bell is a well-known concert violinist and is considered one of the best musicians in the world. In 2007, he was invited to participate in an experiment by (h) *The Washington Post* to play incognito during rush hour in the Washington, DC Metro Station, poised as a social experiment to test context, perception, and priorities. Can ordinary people recognize genius and quality in a different setting?

Bell always performs on the same instrument, a Stradivari, handcrafted in 1713 by Antonio Stradivari during the Italian master's "golden period." The price tag was reported to be $3.5 million.

In 43 minutes, the violinist performed 6 classical pieces considered the most intricate pieces ever written. A total of 1,097 people passed by. Only after 63 people had walked passed did someone finally stop to notice. Only one woman recognized Bell, watched the last 2 minutes of his performance, said hello, and tipped him $20. The final haul for his 43 minutes of playing was a total $32.17. This from an artist whose talent usually commands $1,000 a minute. Bell had just three days prior filled the house at Boston's Symphony Hall where tickets went for $100 each.

In this instance, it did not matter how talented the artist, how expensive the tool, or how revered the music. In the context of playing in a subway, Bell was just another busker. His musical talent was not valued because he was placed in front of an audience who had no appreciation for his artistry or skill. They were not looking to be entertained by such a high level performer, perhaps some did not like classical music anyway. Nor were they in any state of mind to part with their hard earned cash in a hurried state. Instead, Bell is revered amongst classical music aficionados where he regularly plays in concert halls, and his fans are happy to part with $100 or more for a performance.

If we think about context for ourselves, are we placing our work in front of the right audience? Or are we just busking, hoping that someone will stumble across our work and be wowed enough to part with their cash? I think not. In terms of positioning, we need to go where the audience is actively searching out the product we are offering if we are to be valued. Positioning is therefore key to determining price, reach, and effectiveness of our efforts.

Things You Will Need to Build Influence & Authority

Brand Consistency

When you start establishing yourself as an authority, people are going to look you up by your name. If you have Pinterest and Instagram and Twitter and all sorts of social media platforms, ideally it's best to use the same username. When a new platform becomes available (and you have no plan on using them), I still advise that you reserve your username. This applies to your website, too.

If for example, you are in ministry and you want to be nameministries.com, I would get the.org and a.info.net as well. You don't want someone to hijack your brand name by registering varieties of your website. Ideally, usernames need to have no numbers, spaces, or underscores. Keep everything consistent.

Share Valuable Content

Start showing up online and using what you have, and create shareable content like quotes, links, info to other valuable blog posts. If you've got blog posts you've written, go back and repurpose and start re-sharing your old content. Even though you've written it once, new people are hearing about you every day. These are software programs that you can start with a free trial if you want to start easily. Software like Hootsuite, meet Edgar, Tailwind are great examples of automating your marketing funnel. Start with content buckets and start filling them. Use graphics, Scriptures, quotes with your branding.

Use Email Marketing

As an influencer your prospects want to hear from you, so it's important to stay in regular contact. Building an email list that you control is crucial to your success. We will go into more detail in future chapters.

Write a Book

If you are a subject matter expert, or you want to build a speaking or consulting business, writing a book is the best business card you can have! Being a published author is a great way to build your platform and become known as an authority in your market. Writing a book is like having a baby. It's very exciting at first, then the nausea and tiredness of the messy middle sets in, and then it's really painful when you have to birth this baby. Then comes the part of nurturing this baby because it is not going to feed itself. So your business, or book, or project is your "baby". It starts off small and it builds from there.

6

Analogue Days

D o you remember the analogue days? I was born and raised in South Africa during the Apartheid era. I grew up on analogue radio, TV with 3 channels, and Betacam and VHS tapes. My first "official" job was working at an on-air television production company when TV adverts were captured on film and digitized in the avid suite. It was on the cusp of digitizing media with very expensive software and equipment. Watching the behind-the-scenes of television production got me hooked on the medium. I was inspired to learn as much as I could, so in my spare time, I took a presenting and broadcasting class from a well-known news reporter where I learnt how to speak on camera with an ear piece and teleprompter.

The idea of using media and TV to share a message and tell a story was mesmerizing. I pitched my audition tape to as many TV stations as I could, and harassed the producers to take a look at my VHS tape. Alas, it was not meant to be, and after months of rejections, I realized it was not going to be a career option for me. So as a newly married 20-something, I decided I needed to take another route and pursue running my own website design company to pay the bills.

The "bug" for TV never completely left. Once my husband and I had immigrated our family and business from South Africa to England, a small glimmer of hope appeared on the horizon. The local TV station was recruiting for a TV host to interview local businesses, but the catch was that it didn't pay.

Zilch, zero, nada, but hey, you got loads of exposure! Not being one to give up, I jumped on the opportunity to get actual TV experience. That year I spent waking up at 5 AM for shoots and speaking off the cuff with no script (and no budget for wardrobe or make-up) seemed crazy. Considering I squeezed in this moonlighting job while being a mom to a two- and four-year-old seemed ludicrous, but when the "bug" bites and you have a vision of the future, there is no giving up!

The creative entrepreneur in me never sits idle. When the opportunity arose to go to night school to learn digital photography, I jumped on the opportunity. It was the dawn of the digital camera just making its appearance in the market in 2003. The idea of being able to see a photo instantly a moment after it was taken was amazing! It sure beat the smell of chemicals in the dark room. After a year as a part-time adult learner, and another year working with the professional photography association to get my official accreditation, I was set.

At the time, I was working with my husband in his Internet directory business, and using the skills I had learnt in Internet marketing. I transitioned those skills to my new photography business. Very quickly I had a steady stream of clients.

TV experience: check. Photography training: check. Marketing experience: check.

Fast forward 13 years of running a successful photography business, and I hit a wall. A combination of the market changing, stress, grief, burnout, and a traumatic family experience—I ground to a complete halt. I went through a really tough time personally and I just needed to take time out. I closed up shop and became a volunteer in the video production department at Elevation Church in Charlotte, NC. All my previous skills in TV and video production became useful again, and I had found a piece of my purpose.

God used this time to heal me as I took my eyes off of my own situation and was able to do something for others. For a whole year, I volunteered most weekends, with many 5 AM wake-up calls again with no pay. I had a really fun time as there was no pressure, no demands, and no specific goal to achieve other than being willing to serve. It involved working behind-the-scenes, setting up cameras and equipment, firing song lyrics on the computers, supporting the online pastors and talent, and helping to build the online community. Being involved in the church and using my gifts and talents for God, especially when I was feeling low and depressed, was a great way to gather perspective. It was really useful to get out of the echo chamber of my own company, and start to see the needs that are out there.

Mindset Matters

Over the last 25 years of being in business, I have learnt that there are some things that never change. The concept that media, messaging, marketing, photography, and storytelling will always be important in any business or market. However, tools and resources are always subject to change and it's imperative we learn to adapt in order to survive.

As a writer, I'm always interested in stories and figuring things out. At the time of this writing, I have published four books (five when you count this one)—two of which were self-published. The first two were traditionally published by a niche photography-specific publishing agency. I was speaking and teaching on the business and marketing side of photography, and these two books were my first experience as a published author (they are still available on Amazon). Since I've made a shift in my business, what I'm really passionate about now is writing for the Christian Women's Living space and helping other authors publish their own books.

I'm also a branding and marketing strategist and I love to learn new ways of doing things. Because of my marketing experience, I know how to pivot very easily when the market changes or the need arises. I've learnt not to get stuck into old ways of thinking because it's always been done that way. Nor do I allow myself to get comfortable. You can blink and the goal posts will have changed, and a flood of competition would have entered the market.

I'll admit it: I am a course junkie. I've probably spent close to $20,000 over the past 5 years alone on coaching, consulting, and courses. After many hours of reading, watching videos, and taking several courses, I finally figured out the system to self-publishing. Once I took the reins and directed where

I wanted to go, I was able to get some fabulous results. My book achieved 3 Number 1 spots in 3 different categories (Personal Growth and Spirituality, Short Reads, and Women's Christian Living) on Amazon within the first month. I didn't have a publisher, no outside help, and neither did I have a big budget. This was just me figuring it out in the trenches: learning and testing and tweaking.

The reason I share this is because I want to show you that there are things that are out of your control, and there are things that you will always have control over. The industry might change, the tools might change, people might change, but how you show up in the world and share your unique story is entirely under your control.

In the past 25 years I've worked in a few industries, and what I've learnt is that there are foundational truths that will always be important like knowing who you are, whom you serve, and how you show up in the world. The key is to embrace the need for change and boldly take the steps required to move yourself from where you are today, to where you want to be tomorrow. It starts with a shift in your mindset. If you keep telling yourself that your situation won't change, or worse, blame others for your situation, little happens.

By the time this book hits the digital shelves, there could be elements or tools that are already out of date, but we need to start with little steps towards progress. Sometimes, we have the passion and the ideas, but we don't have the necessary tools to achieve our goals. We need to be open minded and get out of our own way.

7

What Publishers & Readers Want

P ublishing is a business. You can reduce the risk of your book proposal being rejected when you have a platform of people to help sell your books. Like any good business, it is in their interest to mitigate the risks. There is an idea that it requires at least 10,000 fans or followers or emails to get a traditional publisher's attention. Their interest is to sell more books and reduce the risk of wasting their time and money so they can scale their efforts. You become less of a risk when you can show a publisher that you have already built a following of fans, readers, and an eager audience.

What Publishers Want

When pitching a book proposal to a publisher, the question they will ask is "Who are you and why should I care?" If you are able to persuade or influence others, then you can consider yourself a thought leader with a platform of influence. This is especially true if you write non-fiction books where readers come to find a solution to their aching problems. Authority, visibility, trustworthiness, reach, and popularity all play into it. This can feel like you are competing in a popularity contest which in essence, you are.

Literary agent (i) Rachelle Gardner says:

"Publishing just ain't what it used to be. Gone are the days when publishers were solely responsible for the marketing of a book. Today's audience is more segmented

than it has ever been before. It's harder than ever to attract people to books. The way to do it is increasingly through personal connection, and that means YOU, the author, making connections with your readers. It has never been more crucial for authors to play a major part in marketing themselves, BUT it has never been easier. If you have major credentials... then don't worry about what I'm saying here. But if NOT.... then you really need to show that you are willing and able to put the time and effort into marketing yourself and building a readership online. You're competing with so many authors who already do this."

If you are interested in pursuing the traditionally published route of securing an agent who will pitch you to a publisher, then you must come prepared and show that you have a platform and are ready to do the marketing legwork.

The Chicken or the Egg?

Many agents and publishers will insist that you have a platform before they will consider representing you. This can seem like a catch-22 situation. How can you be a name in the industry if you have not yet published a book? The reality of the matter is that you *must* start building your platform well before you contact an agent or publisher. Building a following can take years, and the best time to start is now. You don't necessarily have to be "famous" by the time you go to publish, but you do need to demonstrate that you are actively making the effort of gathering a following.

What Readers Want

A (j) survey of 6,000 readers hosted by bestselling author (k) Marie Force offered some eye-opening statistics. Keep in mind that 50% were between the ages of 36-55 years old and 95% of survey respondents were female.

- 88% of readers follow their favorite authors on Facebook.
- 69% of readers use Facebook to find information about their favorite author.
- 86% of readers prefer to buy their books from Amazon/Kindle.

- 35% of readers visit a physical bookstore only twice a year.
- 3% of readers care about the name of the publisher as a seal of approval, where 29% pay some attention and 28% pay no attention at all.
- Readers are 50% more likely to buy a self-published book from an author they already know.
- 60% of readers said that it doesn't matter buying a book from an unknown author.
- More than 32% hear about books they end up buying from Facebook, followed by 12% on Goodreads.
- 60% prefer to use Facebook to get information about their favorite authors, 53% get their info from the author's website, and 45% from the author's email newsletter.
- 56% of reader reviews posted to retail sites sway their purchasing decisions, and 51% of readers feel that reviews are still somewhat important.
- 43% say that a star rating is not that important and they will try a book with a low star rating if they like the cover/teaser/sample.
- Offering a free book makes it 20 times more likely that a reader will be introduced to a new author and buy subsequent books.
- 84% were extremely likely to buy a second book from an author if they enjoyed their free book.
- 70% of readers don't care about seeing "New York Times Bestseller" or "USA Today Bestseller" along the author's name.
- 87% subscribe to the newsletter of their favorite authors.
- 83% of readers like to hear news of new or upcoming releases from the authors they follow.
- 50% said if they really want the book they don't care what the price is, and 23% would not pay more than $4.99 for an eBook.
- 61% said that it does not influence their decision to buy an unknown author's book when they see an endorsement from a well-known author on the cover or blurb.
- 52% said professionalism of the cover design makes the most impact when influencing their purchasing decision.

The good news is that readers care about *you* the author, they want to connect with *you* personally, and they want to hear about your book projects directly from *you*. It shows that readers like to connect with their favorite authors online on places like Facebook, Goodreads, and on the author's own website. It shows that building an email list to communicate directly with your fans is very important. Remember, it's *real people* who read books, so what should be most important to you is pleasing your readers. Having a bestselling status badge doesn't persuade a reader to purchase a book from an author they may not already know, so breathe a sigh of relief; you don't need to sell millions of copies. Since readers prefer all kinds of formats to consume books, it's important to offer all formats like ebook, audiobook, paperback, and hardcover.

In Summary

You can put your fears aside: you don't need a big name publisher to offer you a contract to realize your publishing dreams. Gone are the days of the big publishing houses controlling the access an author has with his/her readers. Today, the reader wants direct access and a personal connection with the author. You can dismiss the idea that self-publishing will be disadvantageous to your sales. The reader doesn't actually care who has published the book, only that it's a good quality and professionally created book they are interested in reading. No matter what publishing route you choose, it is imperative you start building your platform today, so you can connect with your ideal readers and get your message out into the world. If self-publishing is the way you want to go, check out my training (1) Self Publishing Mastermind.

Essential Building Blocks

A platform is not something that you can buy. It's something that you build and nurture over time. You can't build a platform overnight, unless you become an overnight sensation (and that is rare). Buying followers or email addresses does not build a meaningful platform because they won't care about you or your work, and you will just waste your time. Being able to repeatedly reach, speak to and persuade people who know, like and trust you *is* meaningful.

Platform Building is an organic process and will be different for every author. There is no specific formula because it depends on factors like your unique story or message, your strengths and qualities, your target audience, readership and genre.

What is true is that building something of value takes time, effort and placing one brick on top of the other. The basic requirements for all authors (no matter your style or genre your write for) is that you build a strong foundation. This way, with each book published you are able to build on your previous success.

The tools you will need to build your Author Platform include:

- A Signature Author Brand
- A Personalized Website
- Quality of Body of Work (i.e. good writing)
- Email Mailing List
- Social Media Presence
- Press Kit
- Consistency
- Patience

In this book, my goal is to empower you to take action to connect with your audience, and take the reins of your success yourself. We will go into more details in the upcoming chapters, so to help you work through the content, go download my free Checklist at www.mimikacooney.com/platform

8

Write the Right Book

I t can be so frustrating pouring your heart out, bearing your soul, only to have your book tank and launch to crickets. It's book marketing gone bad. For many authors, the problem arises when they spend all the time and effort in writing, only to discover after the launch that they have written the wrong book! Let's look at how you can set yourself up for success by planning your goals and strategy so all your efforts will pay off.

Reasons Why You Should Publish a Book

1. To weave a Personal Testimony or Story of Hope to help and motivate others.

Once you have experienced a life-changing event, you either come out bitter or better. No one wants to read about someone who is still bleeding on the page from their past hurts. It's imperative you work through the process before putting pen to paper. When you've moved through the process of healing and acceptance, then you are ready to share your story.

2. To record some of your Life's Major Events and for Posterity.

Think of your book as a recording of your experiences for future generations to appreciate. If this is your primary goal, then I would consider your book a vanity project. You could pursue the path of self-publishing direct to Amazon or digital for the most cost-effective method. This would allow you to set up a print-on-demand avenue, where you don't have to spend on printing thousands of copies. Instead of having books gathering dust in your garage, you will print as you need them. Some of my favorite resources for this are (m) Draft2Digital, (n) BookBaby, (o) Lulu Press, (p) Ingram Spark, and of course, (q) Amazon KDP.

3. To make some additional Money.

I'll be honest, nobody gets rich on book sales alone, unless you are a celebrity. You need a long-term plan and a robust marketing strategy. You can make a living if you put in the work. Ideally, you want to create a library of at least 20 books and build that over 2 to 5 years. Where the big money lies is thinking of your book as a tool. This will lead to either consulting, coaching, courses, or speaking opportunities (i.e. backend sales).

4. To become a Full-time Writer.

If you have a goal to become a full-time author, then you do need a 5 to 10 year plan and strategy to get you there. You need around 20 books in your collection for the passive income stream to be at a sustainable level. You also need to be serious about building your author platform. Focus on getting your name known and leverage the relationships you have. If you know of celebrities or other big names who can help promote you, it will help to boost your visibility. You will also need to invest in paying for ads through either Amazon or Facebook to continue to grow your audience and drive book sales.

5. To become a Professional Speaker.

Using your book as a tool or business card is a great way of opening doors to speaking. Speaking gigs vary in pay. Take note, that if you welcome an invitation to speak at a church, many churches don't pay at all. However, they do allow back of room sales where you can set up a table and sign books. This works once you've built up a network and a following so people are excited to hear you speak.

6. To establish Authority and/or Grow a Business.

As a subject matter expert you can collate your knowledge into a book. This works as a lead generation tool for your business. They say having a book is the best business card you can have! It elevates your brand authority in a market and creates opportunities. This leads prospects down a funnel toward purchasing your products or more higher-end programs. Self-publishing your own book will ensure you keep control and reap the profits.

The Reality of Publishing

1. Your story does matter, but nobody cares unless it's about the reader. Identifying your target market is key for all future decisions, so you write for the market, versus trying to find a market for your writing. Knowing what market you are writing for is the first piece of the puzzle.

2. The truth is that memoirs or autobiographies don't sell (unless you are a celebrity or are well-known). Many non-fiction writers make this mistake of thinking that they have to tell their whole life story in a chronological manner. Unfortunately, it does not read or sell well. The solution is to think of the life lessons you're trying to share. For example, if you write it more for the Christian Living space as a non-fiction teaching book, you will find a better fit. Focusing on a micro moment or major life lesson works better.

3. Successful book sales is all about positioning and how the book is placed amongst others that are similar. Think of "how to overcome/discover/unlock-

/learn" etc. My own book *Worrier to Warrior: A Mother's Journey from Fear to Faith* started as a memoir but I altered it to fit within the Women's Christian Living category.

4. Self Publishing a book requires an investment of money even if you do it yourself. The key is to do it professionally if you want your investment to pay dividends. You don't want to skimp on a cheap cover or eliminate editing. Conservatively, you could get a professionally designed cover done for $30 to $100. You also need to invest in hiring a professional editor/proofreader before publishing.

5. Authors make the mistake of thinking that by simply pressing publish, that a book will sell itself. The reality is books don't sell themselves. The author is in charge of all the marketing and promotion. This is true even if you get a publishing contract with a big name publisher. They still expect you to do most of the legwork of book promotion. This is why building an online presence (website, social media, email list) is vital for continued success.

6. Nobody cares about your experience unless you make it about how it helps the reader solve their problem. This is especially true when writing for the non-fiction market. If you want to write it simply as a story, then consider it more of a work of entertainment and focus on the fiction market.

So now you have some food for thought. You've got decisions to make about the route you want to take. Once you pick the path, then the steps will become easier.

Next Steps:

- Decide how you want to position your book before you go to the effort of writing the wrong book. Do the research and find the correct category and keywords.
- Finish writing your story and first draft.
- Find a (r) professional editor/proofreader and have them tidy the manuscript to make it print-ready.
- Hire a good graphic designer to create the book cover, or buy a ready-made one on the (s) Book Cover Designers, (t) Creative Market or (u) Self

Pub Book Covers.

- Get to work building your (v) Author Platform and Brand. You need to have your audience primed and ready for when your book launches.

II

Branding Blueprint

9

Branding Blueprint

Many business owners, authors, and speakers who want to put themselves online struggle with the concept of branding. If you gloss over the foundational stage of the branding process, it's hard to put the pieces into place later. There is no point in me teaching you a marketing technique if you don't have your branding right. Understanding who you are, who your audience is, and how you show up in the world is the important first step.

Business First

Building a business and a brand is like building layers to a house. You stack brick by brick, one layer after another. Unless you have the foundation right, it's very hard to build up on a shaky foundation later. This is why I want to encourage you to take the time to design your brand the way you really want it. Once you have complete clarity of who you are, who your ideal client is, and how you show up in the world, it will save you a lot of time, money, and resources. You will get results much faster.

I love this quote from Dr. Seuss: *"Why fit in when you were born to stand out?"* This is what you want to achieve with branding; you want to figure out how to stand out in the crowd, because who wants to be plain, right? By being vanilla is how people, concepts, and businesses get ignored. Unless there is a reason for you to tell your story in a different way, people will think you're just like everybody else. It will not be worth the effort building a brand and a business, only to blend into the crowd. The good news is that you don't have to be like everyone else; you just need to be you and be confident enough to share it!

Why Branding?

Branding is how you stand out in a noisy marketplace. If you are all things to all people, how do people identify themselves as one of your tribe? Branding is how people *feel* about you. It's not just about your brand colors and logos and fonts. That is more of your style sheet, and it helps you keep all your graphics and your visual branding organized. I want to go a little deeper about the more important things—like your core values.

It's how you speak the language of your ideal customer. Branding is perception. Branding is your silent salesman. If you've done a good job with your branding, and you've given people the right message, they will feel good about you. This is what compels them to talk about you to their friends. There is a trust factor that gives them the confidence and reassurance that you're going to deliver. If they've had a good experience with you before, they know that trust is established and you are reliable.

This is why consistency is so important in branding. You can't have your website look one way, and then tomorrow you go and change it up (unless you do a total brand makeover). It's very confusing. This is why you need a branding blueprint to help you decide what is for you and what is not for you. When something comes across your path, instead of being stuck in confusion and being paralyzed by analysis, you will know exactly who you are. When an opportunity comes around, you can confidently say a firm yes or no, without wasting your time. Decide what you do and don't like—you get to choose.

Some questions to help you get started:

- How do you want your day to look like?
- How much time do you want to spend?

- Do you want to be a full-time author?
- Do you want to run a business?
- Do you want to be a full-time speaker?
- Or is this something you want to do on the side?

My personal backstory is that I was a professional photographer for 15 years running my business from home. Eventually, I found that I valued my time with my family more than I did making money from photography. I decided I no longer wanted to work 6 days a week and sacrifice moments on weekends that I could never get back again. I had to change my business model to suit my values. So I switched from photographing weddings on weekends to capturing babies, which I could do during the week. I wanted to work around my kids' schedule, especially when they were little. Even when I got an offer to shoot a big wedding, I politely declined and referred it to someone else without doubt. Knowing my values helped me navigate my business decisions.

If somebody offers you an opportunity, but it doesn't align with your brand and values, you can confidently decline. You're not missing out on some big opportunity if the opportunity does not align with your core values or ideals. I know my decisions have already been made for me. I know down the line, that if I start to say yes when I should say no, it will eventually come back to bite me in the butt. This is especially true when taking on new clients in a business when you just feel that something isn't right. You agree anyway because the money is good. Inherently, it's going to either leave you or the client frustrated. If you feel like you're being undervalued, and they're not paying you enough for your time, it creates resentment. It works the same way if the client feels they're not getting enough value out of you for what they paid. Eventually, everyone feels disappointed. This is why it's so important to know what you stand for from a ground roots level. Then your decisions will be a heck yes or a heck no.

Start with Why

You might have heard of Simon Sinek and his (a) *Start with Why* book. The reason why knowing your why is important is that it will help you navigate the process and refine your reason for doing things. At the end of the day, if you're making choices for the wrong reasons, eventually you can't keep it up. If the only reason that you want to do business or write a book is to make money and make lots of it, eventually it doesn't become a good enough reason. When is enough *enough*? How much money will you need to reach your goal? If you don't have a firm foundation of why you're doing something, you can be very easily swayed to make the wrong choices. Having "making money" as a goal is not a bad motivation. But if it's the only thing that drives your choices, then it's going to be limiting. When you know why you do what you do, you will know where you are going. It will help you get there quicker.

The Why Profile

Having been a self-employed entrepreneur for the last 25 years, I've noticed a theme. I've always had an underlying ethos of offering encouragement, empowerment, and education. Whether I was teaching photographers about marketing, consulting with business owners, helping authors with publishing their books, or working with women in a Bible study, the integral part of who I am has shone through. At the core, I'm a positive minded go-getter with a resilient attitude. I love to encourage others to rise up and be the best that they can be. I love to offer encouragement, empowerment, education, inspiration, and ideas—even if I'm not getting paid to do it.

Think about who you are and how your theme of life has shown up. This will help when it comes to deciding on what market you want to attract. Just because you have an idea for a product or service doesn't necessarily mean that the audience will love it. Are they the kind of people you want to work with? Maybe they can't afford what you have to offer. I've experienced this myself several times where I had to pivot my market choice. The essence of what I offer is very valuable, but if I'm speaking to people who don't see the value or can't afford me, I'm wasting my time.

How can you find an affinity with your audience? Your message will resonate with the right people when they say, "She gets me, she knows what I'm thinking, how did she know?" That is what an affinity means. It's making connections and friendships with people who believe you understand where they are at. They discover that they have things in common with you and they feel like you understand them. That is a meaningful connection.

Here are some questions to help you get going:

- What motivates you to do what you do?
- What do you want to do in terms of freedom of time?
- How much creative license do you crave?
- Why do you have a need for approval?
- Do you want to improve your confidence in a craft?
- Do you want to build a network?
- Why do you want to be respected, be seen as a celebrity, or attain recognition?
- What are your deep needs that drive you to succeed?
- What do you love doing even if you were not being paid to do it?
- What message do you want to convey with your work?
- What are your core beliefs?
- Why do you love being an entrepreneur, an author, a speaker, or a coach?
- What do you love about what you do that motivates you to get up in the morning?

Finding Your Ideals

I love this quote by Dr. Seuss: "*Today you are You, that is truer than true. There is no one alive who is Youer than You.*" The good news is that there is no one else who can be you. As long as you stay true to yourself, you will always make the right decisions. When you feel conflicted or frustrated, it's an indicator that you are making decisions that are not based on your core beliefs, or based out of fear. You try to resonate with someone else's style, voice, or aspirations, then you get out of alignment. What results is content, a book, a business, or a product that is always trying to catch up and keep up with the rules that someone else is setting.

Here is a good exercise to do. It's called a SWOT analysis. On a piece of paper, make four boxes and label them: strengths, weaknesses, opportunities, threats. Now fill in the blank boxes. By defining these aspects of your skill set, you can focus your efforts on your strengths and become a better you. A better writer, a better speaker, a better entrepreneur, a better mom or dad. That is how you shine.

The school system doesn't do a good job at equipping kids to find their strengths, purpose, or calling. It's built to make kids general practitioners. Then we spend the rest of our adult lives trying to figure out that *thing* that we are good at. As adults, we get paid for specialization and being really good at one (or maybe two) things. There is no point in extending loads of time, wasting money and resources on trying to fix your weaknesses. Put that effort into building up your strengths and become the best version of you that you can be. Then ditch or delegate the rest.

As an entrepreneur, author, speaker, coach, or consultant *you are* your personal brand. Your face, your name, and your reputation are on display every single day. If you love to write but you don't necessarily like to sell, then you might need to find someone or something that can help you fill in the gap. If you love speaking and you want to be on stage, then focus on where the opportunities to speak are. If you have an idea for a book or a business, and you know the market has a need for it, it's good to identify your threats or competition to make better decisions. Knowledge is power and sets the stage for success.

If you are still unsure about your strengths or weaknesses, I would highly recommend you do some personality tests. Two of my favorites are the Myers Briggs personality test, and the Standout Profile personality test.

Here are some things to ask yourself:

- What are my personal values?
- What do I value the most? Is it helping others? Is it impact or self-actualization?
- What are my core beliefs?
- What do I stand for?
- What are my boundaries?
- How much time do I want to spend with clients or working?
- How much of myself do I want to give?
- Do I want to be totally out there and become a well-known brand or private?
- What is my heritage, my reputation, and my history?
- What kind of family do I come from?
- What value system did my parents instill in me?
- What is my current mindset?
- Am I confident about my abilities, my products, and my services?
- How do I feel about success and money?

I've worked as a business consultant and I've come to realize that business problems are personal problems in disguise. If we have not worked through the junk in our trunk from our childhood, or gone through an inner healing process, there are little hiccups that will eventually show up. Perhaps it's pride or a lack of confidence or fear that can hold you back. If you have a fear mindset, you might miss out on an opportunity that would stretch you out of your comfort zone. It comes back to staying in your lane and focusing on your strengths. Once you know what your strengths are, then you can start to build your platform and forget about the weaknesses.

Defining Your Client Avatar or Target Market

There is a quote by Zig Ziglar that says, "*If you aim at nothing, you will hit it every time.*" If you don't have something that you're aiming for, you're going to be throwing darts in the dark. Not having a defined target market can cause you to try to please everybody and you end up pleasing nobody. Writing a book for "everyone" is a surefire way of guaranteeing failure. If you're not speaking to someone specific, it's like trying to speak underwater. It doesn't make any sense.

For some, the idea of defining a target market seems as though it could minimize their reach. When I wrote my book on the concept of mindset and anxiety, I knew it had wide appeal and could help a lot of people. But I knew the importance of defining a specific person at a specific time in their life who would resonate with the message. It helped me narrow down my writing and focus to mothers who were dealing with a teenager experiencing severe anxiety. It helped me position my book for continued success.

Who is this person? What are the age demographics? What are her needs? Is she married or not married? These things are important to know because if you understand how to speak their language, they will get you. Never forget that there are "riches in the niches", so focusing in on a market who has the problem will be worth the effort.

If you are a writer, you just need to look at Amazon and all the different categories for books. You have a much higher likelihood of being successful if you narrow down into a specific category for a particular audience. You will be amazed at the different kinds of things on offer. There are categories for knitting, all sorts of arts and crafts, to how to care for Inca lilies. Knowing your target market will help you, especially when you lack money to attract a larger audience. When you niche down and you know who you're aiming at, you can get faster results within a smaller pool of prospects. When you're doing market research and you want to reach a new market, focusing on similar demographics will get you better results.

There is a concept in marketing and business that describes approaching a market either laterally or vertically. A vertical approach focuses on a specific market, industry, trade, or profession. A lateral or horizontal market focuses on offering a broad range of goods and services. Say, for example, you sell shoes and you only want to sell shoes to runners. That would be considered a vertical market. As you come up with new products and ideas, you know you're making shoes only for runners who have very specific needs like weightlessness and agility. It doesn't matter if these shoes would look good on women or children; your focus is on runners. It's better to start with a smaller area and then widen as you get more reach, more finances, and more success.

Some questions to help you define your target market:

- What is her age demographic?
- Where does she live?
- What are her family dynamics? Is she married or single?
- Does she have kids, and if so, what are their age ranges?
- Is she a working professional or a stay-at-home mom?
- Where does she like to shop or go on vacation?
- What TV shows or books does she like?
- What other brands, or businesses and influences is she drawn to?
- What clothing brands does she like to buy?
- What is her spending power?
- What does she value in spending money on?
- Is she a coupon-clipping mom who needs to save money?
- Is she attracted to lavish lifestyle and travel?
- What are her values, beliefs, and ideals that she will not compromise on?
- What communication style speaks to her pain?
- Is she more conversational or formal?
- What keeps her up at night?
- What is her biggest pain point?

If you know what she prefers, then you can find her. This is especially true when you consider Facebook advertising. If you know what she likes, then to reach her, you can target the businesses she likes. Your advertisement is placed in front of the right audience so your money is not wasted.

Finding the Pain

This is another important part of the branding exercise that helps you dig a little deeper so that people pay attention. When you can determine what the biggest pain point is, you can bring the solution to that pain. Think of the difference between a vitamin versus pain medication. A vitamin is good for your health and a nice addition to your health regime. If you miss a day, it's not a big deal. However, if you have a migraine, you suddenly have an urgent need to get rid of the pain. It is causing you discomfort and you cannot focus until the pain is resolved. In marketing, we like to speak to the pain not the vitamin, because solving the pain has much more value. It puts weight on what is important so you can position yourself correctly. Ask yourself this: How am I the solution to the pain? It needs to speak directly to the immediate need to solve the problem today.

Connection

This speaks to a deeper, emotional level of branding. Think about how you *feel* about somebody or about a brand. At the end of the day, we can speak to the mind and our logic, but people still make decisions based on their emotions.

You may notice a lot of the ads these days that focus on lifestyle instead of the actual product. The Jeep TV ads come to mind. It's designed to make you feel like you want to be in the woods smelling nature, or the freedom of the sea breeze in your hair. Oh and by the way, they sell cars. The most successful ad campaigns either make you laugh, cry, or say wow. If you have an emotional connection and feel the experience, you're more likely to remember it. If you can attach an emotion to an event, people will not forget that power of emotion.

Fascination

Sally Hogshead is the bestselling author of the book (b) *Fascinate: Your 7 Triggers to Persuasion and Captivation.* She provides a test on her website called the fascination profile. She has different personality styles based on how others see you, and not necessarily how you think of yourself. It's how you are showing up in the world and how the rest of the world views you. When you're trying to discover your ideal audience, it's useful to know how you are being perceived. Think about what makes you fascinating.

Here are some questions to ask:

- What books, products, and services do you offer that you feel could be of value to provide that emotional connection?
- What benefits or promises do you make?
- If you are offering a solution or transformation, what is the end result that you offer?
- How do you conduct yourself online? Offline and in person?
- How do you answer emails or the telephone?
- How do you show up on social media?
- What are your hard skills, the ones that you've learned on the job?
- What are you good at? What are your soft skills like your personality traits?
- Are you a good listener?
- Are you more forceful or more of a leader?
- What are your unique gifts?
- What things come naturally to you that you can do without much effort?

Think about what actions you take when purchasing something. Most people need a bit of reassurance when they make a buying decision. Sometimes, it takes 4, 5, 6, or sometimes 10 touches before they feel like they trust you enough to part with their cash.

Brand Awareness

This ties into how you show up and how people perceive you. You want to control the narrative of how people describe what you do. When sharing about your book or your work with a friend, there should be consistency in the language that they use. If you've done your branding right, it will all sound congruent. Let's think about how your brand is right now. It doesn't matter where you've been before, you can totally change your direction. Everything from your logo to your messaging, to your fonts to colors. If things have not worked for you and you're just not attracting the right people, you can do a makeover and press the reset button.

Here are some questions to ask yourself:

- How do you feel about your current branding, your logo, your company name, your color scheme?
- Is your current branding authentic to you?
- What does your logo, brand name and colors say about you?
- Describe the words you associate with your work. Are you more traditional, modern bright, moody, artistic, colorful, dramatic, feminine, soft, romantic, fun, graphic, masculine?

All these adjectives will help to describe your style and will be the subtle cues that someone picks up when they look at your book cover or website. If you're not happy with how you are currently being received, you can change it.

A good exercise that you can do is go to Pinterest. Create a board of your favorites: brands, colors, books, scenes, places, people, things, food, furniture, clothing, quotes, etc. Pin things without thinking too hard. When you're not thinking about pleasing anybody, you're just pleasing yourself. You want to look for the common elements and ignore the anomalies. Once you collate your likes, you will start to see a theme and it might be surprisingly eye-opening. This sorts out how your choices stand out amongst everything else. You should start to see a feel, a color scheme, a stylistic point of view.

This will help define your USP, especially your visual brand. You will need branded photography for your headshots for your website, bio, and books. If you are not dressed appropriately in the right brand colors or in the right environment, it doesn't speak to your personal brand. If you are more casual and love soft pastel colors, wearing a dark formal dress in your headshots will not be "on brand".

Velvet Rope

If you've ever been to a restaurant or a fancy club, you might see a red velvet rope controlling access to the VIP area. This concept is important for you to think about as the gatekeeper to the VIP lounge. You only want to give out the golden ticket to the right clientele. This especially applies to a business. If you know there are certain people you want to serve, and others that you prefer not to serve, you can control access. You don't have to bend over and accommodate *everyone* who comes your way. In the same way, you don't have to write books for *everyone*, just the people you feel led to serve. You are entirely within your rights to refuse admission if they do not align with your ideals.

Brand Story

Your brand story is important because your story matters. What part of your personal story do you want to share with your audience? It doesn't mean you have to share *everything*, but I do advise showing a little skin. At the end of the day, you are a personal brand and your face and your name are how you attract people. You need to be able to articulate your authentic story to make that connection. It ties back to affinity—how do they *feel* about you? People want to work with people that they know, like, and trust. The way that you can get them to know, like, and trust you is to share your backstory. This helps your audience to identify themselves in your journey. If you're providing a solution to a problem, then you need to show that you have overcome their problem through experience.

Sharing your story and what you have overcome personally and professionally makes you more real. Sharing your struggles is valuable because there is profit in pain. In other words, even through your own pain you have experienced something hard, but now you have become the overcomer. Just like any good hero story, the audience is rooting for you! Don't feel scared to share the struggles because people love to see the transformation. Through your story they can find a solution and an answer to their urgent problem. People don't buy products; they buy solutions and transformations. If you can show that you will take them on a journey, they will stick with you until the end. Even if you're writing a fiction book, you're writing a story about the hero and taking the reader with you on the journey.

Just like in Hollywood movies, the most successful ones follow the hero's journey. If you can position your reader as the hero, you've won them over. Remember, you're Yoda; you're not the hero. Your reader is Luke Skywalker. You need to take them on the journey. You need to show them through your story that you've got the necessary experience. You want to usher them through this process of empowerment and self-discovery. At the end, they have found the solution and resolution because you have been there to guide them.

10

Understanding Your Marketing Strategy

Now that you know who you are, how you show up in the world, who your readers are, who you want to attract, and who you are happy to say no to, you're ready for the next stage. You've laid your foundation right. The next step is having a marketing plan to direct your action steps. Now that you know where your ideal audience loves to hang out, then you can start creating content that shows up in the right places. Creating content for a particular platform is now easier to do.

Before you start with your content creation, do a little market research. You can easily do this online for free. Things like Survey Monkey or running a poll on Facebook will help you get feedback. People will speak in their own language. If you ask, *"What is your biggest struggle or challenge with X?"*, you'll be surprised what people say. You might think they're having a problem with X, but it actually turns out to be something like Y. This exercise is something I highly recommend *before* you write a book or create a product or launch a business. Do the research first. What is the point of creating content that takes time, money, and effort, and nobody wants it?

For writers, you can call for beta readers before you write your book. If you have a concept or book idea you can pitch it first to see what interests your audience. I have so many ideas for books I want to write, but I'm going to ask my audience first. What do you want to read? What are you struggling with right now that I can help you with? If I bring them into the process early on, they feel like they're part of it. You'll be surprised how they take ownership. So when you come to publish your book or launch a business, they feel like they are one of your co-founders. It really helps to get sales in the door right in the beginning from your raving fans.

A great way of seeing the conversation is what people review. Just reading other reviews of books will give you a plethora of content ideas. If you have an idea for a book and you want to assess if there is a need in the market, just go and read the reviews. Sell before you create. This is especially important if you want to create courses. Have a solid idea before you create the course and see how people buy. If nobody wants to buy and there's not enough uptake in the pre-sell, you can easily refund people their money before you've wasted your time.

If you are an author, a new publisher, or speaker, think of conferences that you can attend. Go to connect and network with people. The more you can be in front of where your ideal audience is, the more you can hear the conversation.

Eventually your brand will be a beautiful-looking building because you've put in all the bricks in the right place. You've built a firm foundation and you know where you're going. Once you have your strategy and your blueprint, then you can put the effort into pursuing the right platforms and go deeper.

How to Know if Your Idea Will Sell

If you're stuck, start with the very first step, a baby step. You can test your content before you commit to a big project. Write a short blog post, ask your audience questions. Invite them to an event. Invite them to download your freebie. You don't want to spend hours and hours in your closet creating something only to have it launch to crickets.

When I was designing the cover for my book *Worrier to Warrior*, I posted the photos from the photo shoot on Facebook. I asked my friends and followers what they thought, and it went gangbusters. I had over a thousand comments of people giving me their opinion. What I thought would be the best option wasn't actually what was the most popular. I went with what was the most popular. By asking the audience, they felt invested in the process, and they were happy to support me by buying the book when it launched.

Sometimes, we can be an island to ourselves because we think our ideas are fabulous. We might think that we have a novel idea, or that we are the first one to come up with it. When you start interacting with other people, you may realize that your idea might be a bad idea. Learn the lesson early so you can you do it differently or make your idea better. I think this is one of the reasons why it can be hard to get a traditional publishing contract. They are so picky about what they want to publish. When you propose a book idea, it may not be about luck or if another author is more favored than you. It's whether or not the idea is sticky and if it will sell. A lot of the time, publishers have the benefit of experience and they know what people are responding to based on their sales data. If an author has an okay book idea but they have already built an audience and an email list, it's more likely they will be offered a contract. Compared to a really great book idea where the author is unknown, it's still too much of a gamble. Good thing you're reading this book so you can become hot property!

Ask the Audience

Think of Hollywood. How many Spiderman movies have there been? How many Marvel comic book movies have been made? Why do we keep seeing the same idea over and over just spun in a different way? The popular ideas become sequels and franchises. History shows that when Hollywood takes the risk once and proves a concept, and it works really well, it's like gold. They know what the audience likes, and once they get traction, they will ride that wave as far as it can go. Think of Star Wars, Jaws, or Star Trek.

Once you understand an audience's habits and buying decisions, it's so much easier and more cost-effective to offer your idea along with it. With any kind of marketing, whether you're an author or a business owner, you are constantly trying to convince people to take a risk. Once you understand what the market wants, it's much easier to position your book or movie that is something that has proven to work. When they pitched the movie "The Lion King" to producers, they pitched it as "Hamlet but with lions".

The important step to take is to do research, and lots of it. Check out what is trending on Google, what is selling on Amazon, and what books are getting the most reviews. Then read their reviews; what are people saying?

11

Personalized Website

I'm sure many of you can testify that it doesn't come naturally to be outlandishly bragful. To tell everybody how wonderful you are can sometimes be hard. Especially for us women, when we're used to being behind the scenes and lifting everybody else up. Sometimes, it's good to take time for ourselves to share what we're good at. I want to take you through a process. It will help you pull out the elements that you need to create a personalized touch that connects with readers on your website.

How to Tell Your Authentic Story without Feeling Cheesy

There comes a time and a place—especially on your own website—that you need to toot your own horn. You need to let people know about you and your accomplishments. I've been monitoring my website visitors, and I have a little app with a heat map that shows where people click on every page. My About Me page is the most clicked page on my entire website! It's the first place people go to when they find my website. They want to know more about me, who I am, and whom I serve. You have an opportunity to connect with your ideal readers by telling them a little bit more about you. If you don't give them enough reason to stick around, they will be gone.

How to Use Words that Sound Like the Real You

We are past the days of English class where "thou shalt speak proper English". We don't do that online anymore. I'm sure my English teacher and you fellow writers would cringe at the thought of not sounding grammatically correct. No matter what we learned in seventh grade, and how they taught us to use conjunctions correctly, that kind of professional speak doesn't have its place online. This is especially true when it comes to being able to connect with people in an authentic way. To create an emotional connection, I would suggest you write how you speak (especially in non-fiction). That is just the plain old truth.

How to Use an Emotional Connection to Inspire People to Take Action

If you don't make the connection with people, you just become words on the screen. You need to use emotional words and you need to position your story so people take action. Whether you want them to email you, buy your program, hire you, or read your next book; inspire them first.

Some questions to ask:

- Are you struggling to describe yourself without feeling cringey?
- Do you feel like your messaging is just not right?
- Is the language not a real indication of who you are?
- Have you tried to put the pieces together of your website and your brand, yet you feel stuck?
- Are you not getting enough clients who are connecting with your work?
- Are you frustrated with the lacklustre response to your writing?
- Do you want to attract passion seekers like you who believe in what you believe?

Many find it hard to talk about themselves for fear of sounding braggy. We are taught not to brag, but to be humble and let someone else do the talking for us. But the truth is, if you don't speak up and tell people about the wonderful work you're doing, how else are they going to know? The same goes for promoting books and works of art. All artists need to adopt a business mindset and approach sharing their message as an integral part of serving others. It's not selling; it's *serving*.

I think it's because you don't celebrate your little wins. You take for granted how far you've come and what you've learned. You're so focused on where you are going that you don't take a moment and say, "I'm glad I'm not where I was last year, and I'm happy I'm taking a great leap forward".

What I've learned is that life is like a walk along a pebble beach. We come across storms, and rocks get thrown at us. We endure the experiences and learn lessons along the way. Every time we learn something new, and go through an experience (good or bad), it's a little pebble. We have the choice to pick it up. If it's a negative experience, we could choose to pick it up and keep it in our backpack, but it will become heavy baggage. If we hang onto it for too long, it will hold us down. I like to think of these life lessons as temporary. I prefer to take the rocks and learn from them, then put them on the ground. They become little pebbles that create a path for others to follow in the dark. Through everything I've learned, even though I might not be the total expert, I can help someone who is perhaps a couple of steps behind me.

How to Tell Your Authentic Story

How would you feel if you had opportunities come your way without you having to be pushy, salesy, or spend on expensive advertising? How do you describe yourself to others? If somebody wants to ask you questions, how will they know that you are the expert? Can you confidently describe what it is you do and how you serve people?

The way that you put yourself out into the world is entirely within your control. If you don't like the narrative of how others perceive you, then change it. We all have our own unique story and that is what makes us different. For many of us, we can feel cringey when it comes to talking about ourselves. We really need to get over ourselves. We need to get over the cringe factor. It's crucial that we get past the fear of telling people our story because our success and the success of those we serve depend on it.

The fear of what people think can hold you back from creating deep connections. When you can push yourself out of your comfort zone and show a little skin, you will be surprised by the reception. People love authentic stories from real people. Don't be afraid to share about your story and journey (the good, the bad, and the ugly). Someone else right now is thinking and praying for the solution to their problem, and you hold the solution in your hands. If you don't show up to the world and be your true authentic self, you are depriving people of what you have to offer. You are discounting the gift and the joy that you can bring to their lives.

When you start being real and authentic, it's very liberating. You don't have to feel like you have to be perfect. Which leads me to another point which is the perfection paralysis. Many of us don't want to take the steps to do the next thing that we know we need to do because we feel paralyzed by not being perfect. You need to decide now, that wherever you are, you just need to start. You need to celebrate the small wins. If you are more confident now than you were last week, that is a win. You've grown and you need to celebrate that.

Your story is the most important thing that can help others. Whether you've survived domestic abuse, or survived divorce, or endured a business failure, or learned a skill that someone else is struggling with, you need to start to see yourself as somebody else's gift. That's where we can start to get past feeling cringey and awkward about what it is that we do. You need to become the mentor and lift someone else up. Like pebbles, you are laying a path for someone else to follow. They don't have to feel like they're stumbling around in the dark because you've been there. It's about a mindset shift and thinking a little differently about what it is that you do and how your story can relate to other people.

Some questions to ask:

- What is your style like?

- How do you like to communicate?
- How do you make people feel when they see your website or your product?
- How would you describe your personality? Is it fun, dynamic, outgoing, warm, moody?

There are a lot of words that make up who you are and how you like to be described. Remember, you control the narrative so decide how you want to be perceived. This is important because once you know what your style is, then you can marry your style with finding your ideal audience. When you feel that you can connect with similar people, it creates resonance. Then it doesn't become selling but simple communication. Once you know what it is that you want to do and what it is that you offer, you can be clearer. Clarity trumps being clever, so the clearer you can be, the better.

Finding Your Ideal Target Market

We can't be all things to all people. If you think that you can help everyone with your book, then you are not speaking to anyone. If you aim to please everyone with a pulse and a credit card, you'll end up pleasing no one (including yourself). You need to speak to a single person, just like you would having a conversation over coffee.

A good exercise to determine your ideal audience is to think about her as a real person. Give her a name. What is her age? Where does she live? Where does she like to shop? What songs does she like to listen to? Where does she like to go on vacation? What kind of clothing style does she like? What are her family values? What does she believe in?

Once you've determined who she is, you can position yourself to be available where she likes to shop and hang out. When you've strategically placed yourself in the right circles, the right people (who believe what you believe) will find you and connect. Instead of you trying to be what you think people want you to be, you can just be you.

When clients come to me for business advice and they ask if they should use Facebook ads or Google ads, LinkedIn or YouTube, I say stop. You are asking the wrong question. We need to backtrack and first figure out who you are speaking to. Once you speak the right language in the right place, then you can identify what tactic or tool is going to be the most effective.

Just because "everyone" else is doing video, or paid ads, or book trailers doesn't mean you should. Is that what your target market wants? Save yourself a ton of time and effort, and only use tools and tactics that will get you close to the right people. Suddenly your message becomes a dog whistle at a pet show and everyone comes running.

If you can't figure out what your message is in the first place, it's hard to position yourself. What do you want to be known for? Do you want to be a health coach who loves to help moms? Do you want to be a business mentor who wants to help people start a business? You need to decide what it is you want to be known for, and put your flag in the sand and own it. Be known for something. Once you pick a spot in the sand, everything becomes much clearer.

Sometimes, it's hard to separate the person from the project or the product. "I'm an author" or "I'm an artist" or "I'm an entrepreneur". Those are "doing" words, not necessarily what your *thing* is. Once you know what makes you unique, what makes you passionate, then you can figure out what makes you good at what you do. Then you can really own it and people can connect with you on a deeper level. Everything from social media posts to the way you describe yourself online needs to be congruent with your core. What do you stand for?

Use Words that Sound Like the Real You

We need to write the way we speak and just be real! I know, I know, the writer in you is probably cringing at the thought of not using correct sentence structure. However, there comes a time when it's not useful to be perfectly poised with punctuation. When talking to me in person, you will find that I like to use weird words like "fabulicious" or "chillax". It's how I am authentically and how I want to come across to a stranger who has never met me. I don't want to appear as inauthentic by trying to be "proper" online or in my writing, and then something else in person. My style of writing is just how I speak, and it creates a deeper connection with my readers when they feel they are getting to know me. You need to be your authentic self. That doesn't necessarily mean that you have to air your dirty laundry for the world to gasp at. Everything has already been invented. Nothing is new under the sun. So how do you stand out in a crowded and busy market? You shine what your mama gave you, which is the you that only you can be!

What Your Bio Needs

There are three sections to your bio that you need to have:

1. You need to have a **mission statement**. This helps people to connect with you on an emotional level. What is it that you believe? What are your values? Your mission is to help people, so write how you speak. What makes you different is that you're not selling a product, you are selling your personality. By having a mission statement, people know what it is that drives you so they can find resonance in your story. It's also how they exclude themselves when they realize they are not a good fit. This is a great way to help you avoid dealing with people who are not your ideal readers/clients. If they know what your mission is and they don't agree with your mission, then you've saved yourself a ton of time.

2. You need a **formal bio** written in the third person. This is how someone would introduce you on stage if you were speaking or how a podcast host would introduce you. You can list awards, accomplishments, press mentions and experiences. Just like your resume or CV, but written in a story format. This is important, especially if you want to be interviewed by the press and be seen as the expert. You want people to know that you're credible and why they need to hire you. It needs to be concise, to the point, and written in short sentences.

3. You need to have an **informal bio** written in the first person. Just like you are speaking to your friend or creating an online dating profile. How would you describe what it is that you've done in the past? Some call it

your elevator pitch. Create an emotional connection by describing your values and some personal interests.

Personal Brand Photography

Your About Me or Bio page is usually the first place people click when they find your website. Besides your written bio, the next most important aspect is your visuals. Potential readers and clients need to put a face to a name to build that trust factor. You need to have a professionally shot headshot photo that is crisp and clear. It's imperative that you use a good quality photo so ditch the selfies. In the same way that body language speaks louder than words, your photos and visuals speak to the quality of your work. Think about it: if you can't be bothered to get a professional headshot done, perhaps your writing is less than professional? It's the same psychological concept when it comes to book covers. Your imagery, the style, the quality, and the colors all speak to your brand style and quality.

My experience as a professional photographer spans 15 years. I've worked with clients to help them make over their brand style and image. They were able to go from begging for clients to work with them, to having a waitlist overnight just because their website and imagery reflected quality. They were already producing great work, useful services, and a wonderful book; they were just not positioning and packaging themselves right.

I would suggest hiring a local professional photographer who can give you a variety of poses. Think about sitting, standing, close-ups, head and shoulders, and some lifestyle natural poses. Think about your style and color of clothing—do they match your brand? Ditch your favorite sweater and go for solid colors that won't date in years to come. Think less is more; think clean, stylish, and classic.

How you pick a good photographer is to look at the light in the subject's eyes. Can you see the color of the eyes? Are they clear? Forget about black eye sockets that do not translate well. Avoid dark or busy backgrounds that detract from your face. Avoid distractions like trees sticking out of your head, overhead fans, or telephone poles.

When you have your proofs back, choose one head and shoulders close-up as your go-to profile photo and use it *everywhere*. Make sure the color of your eyes is lively and preferably something with you smiling. Showing a little teeth makes you look approachable and translates well. So forget about the artsy looking shots of you looking in the distance, looking moody, or if your head is cut off (too close is not good either). It's not about the shoes or the outfit; it's all about the "feels".

The Press Kit

If you want to position yourself as an expert and get invited as a guest on TV, podcasts, radio and blogs, you need a press kit. If someone is interviewing you, how would they introduce you? If you are a speaker on stage, how do you want the host to describe you? This is where that list comes in handy. What education you've had, what awards you've won, what experiences you've had, give them a reason why they should listen to you. Why are you credible? This is where you need to demonstrate that you know where your value lies.

If you are approaching magazines or podcasts or you want to be featured as a guest blogger, you have to show what's in it for them. How will your experience and your expertise help their audience? Nobody cares that you've written a book, but they do care if the book will help a person achieve something or overcome a problem. Say, for example, that you are a health practitioner and you want to write a story for a local newspaper. You want to make sure that you are writing for the health section and offering helpful tips. Your story would not fit in the general section; it needs to be specific. The health editor will be able to pick up your press release and know that you've got a good hook, a unique angle, and a credible story. If it has a good point of view, they might feature you.

If you are a speaker or an author and you want to share about your latest book project, you need to provide something useful. I've been a podcast host since 2013 and one of the things that grates my cheese is when an author pitches their book to me without having done any research. They treat it just like another press mention, and send out a mass email or offer a story that is irrelevant to my show. Don't be *that* person. You'll get deleted or added to the slush pile very quickly.

Provide information so the podcast interviewer knows that you're there to offer value, not to sell something. Don't expect to just talk about your book and how wonderful it is; that is called an advert. Podcasts are conversational so treat it like you're chatting with a friend. Don't think it's a monologue where you have to keep talking. Give the host a second to interject and ask questions. Many trained speakers find this hard because they're used to holding the attention of the room for a long period, and think podcasts work like that, too. It's not a sales pitch but an opportunity to share your story through a two-way conversation.

One Pager

Make it easy for the media to find your info by emailing your bio, your headshot, and your topics of discussion. Don't send links to your website and expect them to search for the info. Don't be lazy; be professional. In the media industry, we call this your One Pager (usually a printable PDF). It contains your formal bio (in third person), your talking points, your contact info and social media links, along with your headshot photo. Remember, keep it to one page; that is why it's called a "One Pager". You can mention "As seen on" if you've been featured on other big name publications. Keep it short, punchy, and to the point. Include the text version of your bio in .txt or Word.doc format so they can easily copy and paste it into the post or story. You're making it so much easier for the media to work with you, which improves your chances of success.

Talking Points

What topics can you cover and why is it worth interviewing you on the subject? By listing your topics of discussion, you help to give the media story ideas. If, for example, it's a marketing podcast, show them how you're an online marketing expert through a story of client success. Using topics that start with "how to" e.g. overcome, achieve, realize, learn, uncover, discover, lose, gain, etc. do really well. Like "How to lose 10 pounds in 10 days after a Thanksgiving Binge" is specific and relevant if you pitched it during that specific season.

You may think that you could never make it onto one of those big publications, but where there is a will, there's a way. If you can provide something of value, consistently show up and make yourself available, and you don't give up, you will succeed.

Quality of Work

"You can't put lipstick on a pig." This is a British saying which means you can't make something that is ugly look pretty just by dolling it up with lipstick. If the quality of the product is bad, or the quality of the book is below par, then no amount of marketing can sell it. You have to start with a good product. This is why you need to master the craft of writing before you even think about publishing. I know this sounds obvious, but believe me, I've read so many badly written books because the author didn't take the time to craft a top-notch product. The resulting poor sales were a reflection of that. Readers will let an author know if their writing stinks by leaving bad reviews, and this can sting for first-time authors. This behavior has given self-publishing a bad rap. Rookie writers hastily upload a book and forget to check if it's good enough quality to be there in the first place.

Before I can help you with marketing and promoting your book, you need to get it written for publication quality. This goes for editing, too. Don't skimp on paying a professional editor and proofreader to go over your work. The final manuscript needs to be polished with correct grammar, spelling, sentence structure, punctuation, capitalization, etc. Even if you're a great writer, you still need a fresh set of unbiased eyes looking for errors. I'm sure you have well-meaning friends and family who are happy to read your book for you. However, they should not be considered reliable if they're not familiar with editing for publication. Make the investment and find someone who can clean it up for you. The entire book project can tank if readers discover errors and you get bad reviews.

There is an enormous amount of resources available to help you become a better writer.

Some of my favorite writing resources include:
   (c) Jerry B. Jenkins Writers Guild
   (d) Serious Writer
   (e) Hope Writers
   (f) Masterclass

III

Email Marketing

12

Build an Email List of Raving Fans

About 5 years ago, I hosted my podcast show on a platform called Blab. It's where Google Hangouts meets live video before the days of Facebook Live. I hosted weekly live interviews where I could chat directly with guests, interact with comments from viewers, and build up followers. Long story short, Blab went under due to a lack of funding. Everything I had built up went poof, gone, in a matter of minutes. The worst of it all was that I had no way of gathering the contact info of the followers I had built up, so I had to start all over again.

It goes to show that the likes of YouTube, Instagram, Facebook, and even Amazon can change overnight without warning. Consider Facebook: when the algorithm suddenly changes, people complain about their lack of reach. With social media, you are just borrowing someone else's platform. This is why it's so important to get prospects off social media and onto your email list. Once you have someone's email, you have a direct line to be able to communicate with them.

Besides your own website, the only content you own is your email list. You need your own website with a custom domain (preferably in your name or brand name). Try to steer away from free hosted websites like www.yourname.freebly.com that use an obscure domain address. To look professional, you need a domain that you own like www.yourname.com, so you will have to pay for hosting. There are many affordable options for registering your domain like GoDaddy or Bluehost. You don't need to be a website designer to create a good looking website; there are so many easy-to-use templates. Even if you have just one page and you collect somebody's email, that is all you need. This is called a landing page where the one and only thing a visitor can do is enter their email address.

Why Email?

Forget about the things you've heard about email being so last season, that people are too busy to read emails. I can tell you—email is still king! People check their emails every single day as a matter of habit. Email is one of the communication methods that is personal to everyone. This is why people are very protective of their email; no one enjoys receiving spam. It's important to incentivize prospects to proactively join your email list by invitation only. You cannot add their email address to your list without their permission. With today's strict GDPR rules in Europe, email service providers are even more particular about avoiding spam complaints. So forget about adding those emails manually that you got from the pile of business cards sitting on your desk, or from that networking meetup. You must have prospects express permission and have them opt in themselves. This is why it's called "permission marketing", as you need to have their express permission to contact them. You can control the content you send out in your email newsletter, and it's up to the reader to decide to read it or not.

How we incentivize prospects to join our list is by offering something of value. When people sign up for your email list and you are providing value, you are serving them. So don't think of it as being salesy. You are serving them by offering them value in their email inbox. Offering a freebie and incentivizing them to join your email address list is an ethical way of getting permission to communicate with your readers (aka called the "ethical bribe").

Reasons to Use Email Marketing

Research

Email opens a two-way conversation. If you're thinking about a new book idea, you can email your readers and host a survey. Asking your fans first before you launch your next big book idea could save you from wasting a lot of time and money.

Book Reviews

As an author with a new book, you need an email list to drive your sales and to encourage reviews. Using email is a great way of asking for reviews. You don't know who the people are who buy your books since Amazon does not share that information with its authors. Once your book is launched, you can follow up several times to encourage that the reviews are added.

Content Plan

There is no need for you to get overwhelmed with crafting compelling content every single day. Buy yourself an assistant by scheduling it to auto-post in software like Hootsuite, MeetEdgar, or Tailwind. You can sit down in one day and design a spreadsheet of ideas and create eye-catching content for free with software like Canva.com. You could create themes for particular days of the week and schedule your posts to upload automatically, while you get a massage or sip Piña Coladas on the beach.

Email Marketing Must-Haves

1) Email Software

You need an email program or CRM (client relationship management) software. You can start with a free option like MailChimp or Mailer Lite; or more sophisticated options like Active Campaign, Drip, Constant Contact, Get Response, Convert Kit, Aweber, etc. Several of them offer a free trial or a free number of subscribers before they start charging. You can always switch at a later stage if you need more flexibility with tagging and more custom options. Using a landing page on your website or a popup tied into your CRM is a great way of capturing those emails. Most software offers the ability to add a pop-up or sign-up box on your website with easy copy and paste HTML code.

2) Freebie, Lead Magnet or Ethical Bribe

Whether it's a free chapter of your book, a checklist, study guide, printable, devotional, video series, audio book, or coupon code, pick something that speaks to your audience. You're not going to give somebody the whole pie right up front. You're going to give them a taster, a piece of the pie. I like to think of the Freebie like a piece of a bigger pie. Think about it as a start to the conversation, then you continue the conversation with an email welcome sequence. Create something that is eye candy with color that pops. You can design something gorgeous for free in Canva.com using their drag and drop feature and free stock images. You can create a document in Google drive and export it as a PDF, JPGs or PNGs image files. The most popular formats are a PDF because they are easily read on mobile devices.

3) Landing Page or Pop-up

A landing page is a static page that people land on when you want them to sign up for your email list. The effectiveness of a landing page is that it has just one function—to get the prospect to complete the form with their email address. No links, no browse buttons, no rabbit holes. They can't do anything other than sign up.

You can create a landing page on your website or use a program that creates one for you like LeadPages. Ideally if you use Wordpress, you can create a separate page through your own domain using a plugin like OptimizePress. Using a pop up feature through your email CRM provider is a great way of capturing leads when visitors are reading your blog posts. It's very easy to set up. You simply copy and paste the embed code for the form on your website and it pops up when a new visitor lands on your website. This triggers the start of your email sequence.

4) Email Welcome Sequence

A missed opportunity that you want to avoid is having prospects sign up and download the freebie, then they don't hear from you again. Without regular contact they quickly forget why they signed up in the first place and they are more likely to unsubscribe. You need to create what we call a welcome sequence in your email program to keep warming them up. Ideally sending an email once a week is a good idea, but if you can only manage once a month that is fine, too. Remember, consistency is key.

13

Create a Freebie Offer That Hooks Readers Fast

C reating a freebie or sample offer is integral to building your platform. Without something to offer people, there is no reason for them to opt in to your email list. Asking people to sign up for your newsletter is not enough of an incentive. People are busy and don't want another to-do.

The key is to start with something small. Think about the last time you tried a new bakery or ice cream store. Before you were aware of what they had to offer, you might have been persuaded to try their new fancy flavor. Everyone loves a bit of a taste, right? A prospect needs to follow a path for you to take them to your desired result. In other words, if you want them to buy your book, you need to start with the end in mind. Think of where you want them to go. What is the first touch you want them to have with you?

What we are doing with a funnel is giving them one little thing, which leads to another thing, and then to another. Call it micro commitments. When you are taking people on a journey, you need to start with small steps.

How to Create a Freebie / Lead Magnet

The first thing you need is a freebie offer, or what we call a lead magnet or ethical bribe. What can you offer for free that is easy to download and consume? Popular options are a printable PDF (2 to 3 pages in length), prayer cards, printable checklists, devotionals, screensavers, etc. The key is to give your prospects something that they can't get anywhere else, that you only offer on your website. It could be a product that is available for purchase in your store, as long as there is a perceived value to it with a price tag. People don't value free, so showing that there is a value to it will make it more enticing.

One of my favorite tools to use for design is Canva.com. You can create some really professional-looking images, and it is very easy to use. You don't need any major graphic design skills. You just need an eye to make sure it looks good. It provides templates which will speed up your workflow.

It's important to create something that your audience wants, preferably a piece of your higher priced product (i.e. your book). In this case, offering the first chapter or an accompanying devotional, journal, or PDF checklist are great freebies. Remember, though, that you can create the prettiest looking offer, but if it doesn't lead to the next step in your funnel, it is pretty much a waste of your time. Make sure they relate to each other.

The way you figure out what your audience wants is by hosting a survey or poll to determine the felt need. In the author's space, we talk about the felt need in terms of what your audience is thinking and feeling that you could speak to. This doesn't have to cost you any money. If you have an email list, you can survey them, or if you have a Facebook group, you can pose a question. If it's not your group, just be careful that you don't come across as spammy, as you don't want to appear to be selling anything. You just want to ask questions or pay attention to what people are already talking about in the groups.

Format of a Freebie or Lead Magnet

When you create your freebie offer, I would advise making it a PDF since it is easy to email and download because the file size is small. This format works on all devices and is easy to print. You don't want to offer your epub or mobi version that you get when you export your book. Make it easy for readers to consume your content; remove any barriers. An ebook, checklist, worksheet, study guide, audiobook, screensaver are some ideas for freebies. Think of something that relates to your products. It needs to be a quick read, something they can read within 5 minutes. You can use templates to create something quickly so all you need to do is customize your fonts and colors.

How to Fill the Funnel

With so much digital noise, you need to touch people at least 7 to 10 times to be heard. Whether it's a Facebook post, or a Tweet, or a paid ad, you have to consistently post for people to become aware of you. This is why you need to create brand awareness and why consistency is so important. To find those raving fans, you need to start at the top and get prospects into your funnel. There is no point in putting effort into attracting people who are not the right fit as you're both going to end up frustrated. By the time they get to the bottom of the funnel, they need to be in the right place.

So how do you attract the right people in the first place? Before you start any kind of promotion, it's important to know who you're speaking to and where they hang out. We covered this in the Branding Blueprint section. Once you have a blueprint of who the prospects are, you can aim and hit the target.

There are so many social media platforms and methods that you could spend your time spinning your wheels. There is no point in pushing your Instagram feed if that is not where your people are. Pick three platforms and get a taste for how they work. Eventually, you will find one that works for you and you've found your golden nugget. I have a social media presence on all platforms. I have a Pinterest account, a Twitter account, a YouTube channel, and Instagram, but I don't necessarily spend a lot of time there. I spent the majority of my time on Facebook because that is where I've had the best interaction. Don't feel overwhelmed as if you have to be everywhere to be effective. You just need to think about where your readers and your audience are, and go with that.

No matter what platform or social media method you use, you still need to drive them back to where you can control the conversation, which is email. One thing to keep in mind is that you need to drive at least 3, probably 5 times more traffic to the top of the funnel to provide you with results. So if you want 10 new readers, you've got to work backwards and understand that you probably need to attract 100 prospects. As they move along the funnel and you shake the tree to filter them, not everybody's going to be your ideal reader. That's okay as long as you know that you're going to be putting a lot more effort at the top. Then by the time they get to the bottom, you only need to deal with a smaller amount of leads.

In Summary

This whole Freebie system works as your funnel and keeps things working while you sleep. This is how you build your email list on autopilot. This is how you sell books while you're sleeping because this system works for you. All you need to do is set it up, put the few little pieces in place, and have it flow into an email sequence. Your readers are excited that they are able to get more content from you. So just keep cranking out those books, keep filling your programs, and give them more good content. The more valuable content you create, the more it just keeps building. That is how people sell lots of books. If you look at some of the bestselling authors who are selling loads of books, they have a system and they work it to their advantage. So don't expect overnight success. Take the long-term approach and build each step, each book, and each launch as a building block to your success.

14

Landing Pages

A landing page is a single use page on your website (or hosted through a third party). It is used for one thing—to get people to take a single action. Landing pages are mostly used to encourage readers to sign up for your email list, join a waitlist, or purchase a product. The reason they work so well is that they eliminate all confusion about the intended action the reader is meant to take. There are no links to a blog or social media, and no other ways for visitors to get distracted. It's one call to action, and one button or link. If you have a Wordpress website, it should be fairly easy to set up a landing page, or you can install a plugin like (a) Optimize Press.

For writers, we already know that building our email list is imperative. So it is important to have a landing page for readers to join your list and get access to your freebie. I personally prefer to have a different landing page for each of my books so I can better monitor which books are the most popular.

Once readers click the button to sign up, they are taken to a form to fill in their name and email address. Then they are taken to a thank you page. Having a specific thank you page after a reader signs up is crucial to monitor that the reader actually took the action. If you use Facebook ads, the pixel code can be added to this thank you page, and for Google analytics, it will better monitor your clicks.

The third part to a landing page, which is optional, is what we call the "tripwire" page in the marketing world. The tripwire is where you're able to make an offer, before offering the "thank you, please confirm your email address" page.

Think about it: once they have clicked to join your list, they are most interested in what you have to offer within the next 10 minutes. Therefore, it is important to offer them a way to take immediate action. This is called the upsell. Offer something enticing like a special discount to another book or product or service, thereby covering the cost of any advertising you might have spent. With a tripwire page, you offer either a Yes or No option; if they click Yes they are taken to order, or No takes them directly to the thank you page. Once the reader arrives at the thank you page, you provide them with what you originally promised (the freebie), and/or to follow you on social, share the page with a friend, links to other books, join a Facebook Group, etc.

Landing Page Flow

- Step 1: Reader finds your landing page/offer and clicks button to sign up.
- Step 2: Reader is taken to form to fill in email and name.
- Step 3: Reader is taken to tripwire page where you offer an upsell.
- Step 4: Reader opts Yes or No. Yes take them to the order/purchase page (followed by the thank you page), No takes them directly to thank you page.
- Step 5: Reader arrives at thank you page and clicks to download the freebie.
- Step 6: Reader clicks to confirm the email they receive.

Once they have taken the sign up action, they have triggered the start of your funnel and the automated sequence takes over. In the welcome email, they should have the option to click to confirm their email address. This is called a two-way authentication to ensure they intended to sign up with the strict anti-spam rules. Sometimes, this email finds it way in their spam folder, especially with Gmail because it's overzealous with reducing spam. I like to remind people on the thank you page to please click to confirm their email, and check their spam folder if they don't receive the email, and to whitelist my email address (so they receive future emails). This way, I'm covering my bases if the email falls through the cracks. Many CRM programs won't start the automated sequence or trigger the funnel until the reader confirms, so make sure to encourage this action.

Always think of what action you want readers to take. Some people would argue that I have too many pages for them to click on, but research has shown that it works.

15

Email Funnels that Sell while you Sleep

P
eople are using cellphones to order products, communicate, connect, be entertained, and read books. It seems that hardly anyone is reading paper magazines anymore. The same goes for watching TV. Who has time to watch ads these days? I prefer to glue my finger to the DVR and press fast forward so I can watch what I'm interested in. Times have certainly changed. As a consumer, I dictate how and when I'm open to receiving information. If I sign up for an author's offer while sitting on my sofa at 10 PM, I want access to it immediately. You're busy, I'm busy, I get it. Nobody's got time to be sending out individual emails and following up with people 24/7 so we have to maximize our time.

If you find yourself consistently doing repeatable tasks, then it's time to automate the process. An email funnel is something you set up and leave on autopilot. It's one of those things where you put a little bit of effort in the beginning, and then just let it do its work. Once you have the funnel working, you can tweak it, and rinse and repeat. It's really that fabulous!

What Is a Funnel?

Businesses know the importance of filtering prospects so they arrive at the intended destination (aka the sale). They cannot waste their money and resources on prospects who are not the right fit. As an author, it's important that you be very specific when speaking to your ideal reader, so you don't waste your time or resources.

Think of a funnel in stages. It starts with awareness and making the reader know that you exist, just like you would when walking past a shop window. Then you filter them down by interest, just like you would entice a shopper through your door by displaying eye-catching products. Then you need to figure out exactly what their need is so you can offer them the right style, size, and color. Once they try it on and it's a good fit, viola! The sale is made!

Through that filtering process, you're moving them further into decision-making. They get to pick if what you have to offer is of interest to them. Then they will take action. Now of course, you end up with less people at the bottom of the funnel than at the top. Don't be scared if you end up losing email subscribers; that's exactly how it's meant to work. You are filtering them so you can find your hot leads and eager buyers.

The Automated Email Marketing Sequence

An automated sequence is like the yellow brick road. You are taking them down a path that will lead them to where you want them to go. This is why it's important that you decide in advance exactly where you want them to go, then you work backwards. Do you want them to buy a book, a product, or a course? Where do you want them to end up at the end of your funnel? If you know you want them to buy your book, how do you help them make a decision to get there?

Online marketing is like dating. You wouldn't go up to someone and ask them to marry you the first day, right? You want to introduce yourself and allow them to get to know and like you. Then they can decide if it's going to be a good fit. Through the email follow-up sequence, you're going to be specific to weed out those that are not interested. By asking a series of questions or offering them other products or books, you move them along the funnel.

Most email marketing programs like MailChimp, Active Campaign, or MailerLite offer the feature of automation, sometimes as an extra upgrade. It really doesn't matter what email program you use, just that you have this automation option. Once people have opted in, the first email you send is a welcome email. This is where you give them what they signed up for. Then the beauty of the automated sequence kicks in.

With a funnel, the objective is to turn what we call cold leads (people who don't know you yet) and filtering them into hot prospects. When cold leads haven't heard of you before, you need to build the relationship and offer value to warm them up. Sharing parts of your story is a great way to show a little skin and build affinity.

Don't get concerned that you're putting all this effort into gathering emails and many prospects unsubscribe. That is okay because not everybody is going to be interested in what you have to offer. You will have to pay more for your email provider if you have more emails, so eliminating those that are not the right fit will save you money in the long term. I like to purge my list from time to time to keep it clean and up-to-date. After I've done a book launch, and I know I've emailed people quite a few times, I do a cleanup. If they have not responded to my last 10 emails I delete them. If they haven't opened or clicked on an email or taken action within the past 6 months, I delete them. I don't want to be paying for time-wasters.

I would rather have a thousand true fans who actually open and read my emails, and purchase my books, than having an inactive list. Time is money. You're spending time on creating content for people you want to serve. You want to make sure that you're speaking to the right audience. So don't be scared if you lose people. The more emails you have in the sequence, the more likely people will unsubscribe. That's okay because again, you are filtering them down.

You can expect a 30% sign-up and open rate. What this means is out of 100 people you reach, maybe only 30 of them will actually sign up to join your email list. Of those 30%, another 30% might open your emails and actually take action. So you really are looking at a much smaller percentage compared to when you started. This is why email list building is a continual process.

16

How to Setup a CRM

A CRM refers to a Client Relationship Management system that helps you manage and organize your contacts. It's usually a subscription that you pay for monthly. Some of my favorites are: (b) Active Campaign, (c) MailChimp, (d) Mailer Lite, (e) Drip, (f) Constant Contact, (g) Aweber, (h) Get Response, (i) Mad Mimi, etc. I personally use Active Campaign because of their affordability and funnel tagging feature. They all vary in price and functionality so choosing one depends on your budget and what functionality you need. For the purpose of setting up an automated email sequence, I suggest starting with MailerLite because email automation is part of their free plan (but is subject to change).

One important aspect to remember is with the new GDPR rules that have come into effect, you have to be careful of spamming your audience. You cannot just take someone's email address and plug it into your email program manually. You have to have users opt in themselves because the email programs record their IP address. An IP address is basically how the Internet records your location from your computer or cellphone. Wherever you are in the world, your IP address identifies you. If the actual user and their actual location don't add up, it can be flagged as suspicious and spam.

When creating your email follow-up sequence, start with email 1 which is your welcome email. Then send 3 to 7 emails spread over the next 7-14 days, ideally 2-3 days apart so it's not too frequent. If your goal with writing a book is to build a speaking career, or to get consulting or coaching clients, then you have a higher investment at the end. You might want to consider extending your funnel duration so you can overcome objections. If all you're interested in is building your email list to sell more books, you don't have to give them your life story; just enough to gain their trust. Books are inexpensive ranging from 99 cents to $30, so giving enough info to build the author/reader relationship goes a long way to building a true fan.

How you create an email conversation is just how you would have a telephone conversation, or a conversation while sitting in front of someone at a coffee shop. What would you say to them to pique their interest? What can you offer them as an incentive once they've downloaded your book? Perhaps drive them back to your blog or to an article that is related to the topic you've talked about. Or maybe a story of interest about what someone else is doing. Don't be shy about recommending other authors, books, and products if you feel it will serve your audience. It doesn't have to be all about you trying to sell to them 24/7.

When you have your email program set up, you want to have an opt-in sequence that flows like this:

Email 1: Day 1 - Welcome

Hello, welcome. Thank you for downloading X. Here's your free gift. Ask a question.

You don't want to be in their face. Waiting 2-3 days in between emails is perfectly fine.

Email 2: Day 3 - Follow Up

Hi, checking up on you. How did you enjoy the freebie offer? If you enjoyed the book, I really would love a review. Click here to read the reviews that we've already received.

You can offer another freebie or complementary products.

Hey, by the way, I've got this extra book for you that you might like. Click here to get your free copy (or discounted offer).

Constantly give them gifts because there is a concept called reciprocity. When you're giving somebody something, they feel obliged to give something back. If you've given them a gift in the form of a book, they're going to feel obliged when you ask them for a favor in return. Reviews are super important, so they're going to feel obliged to do that for you since you've been so generous.

Let me say one thing about reviews. People will say they will review your book, but maybe only 30% will actually take the time to do it. So just build that into your planning. I learned this the hard way and got very upset when people said they would review my book and they didn't. Sometimes they just don't have the time, or perhaps they didn't like the book and they would rather not say anything. That's fine, too, but I encourage honest reviews. I want people's honest feedback so I know how I can make things better next time.

Email 3: Day 5 - Review & Follow Up

Hello, Here is a story about when I .... Here is a lesson I want to share, etc. Would you be so kind as to leave a review of my book (insert link)?

Again, you want to drive them back to your website (like a blog post) so they get to know, like, and trust you. Continue to offer valuable content. Then you can gently remind them to leave a review.

Email 4: Day 8 - Offer (Hard Sell)

Hello, how have you enjoyed XYZ? If you struggle with X I have a solution... Check out my offer of (link to your website)...

Eventually, you can offer them something with a higher investment like a coaching call, a course, or a product. I write for the non-fiction business/-marketing space so I like to offer consulting, courses, and a membership site as additional offers. I want readers to come back and to feel confident and comfortable with me, so that they'll want to invest in something more. I regularly provide additional free content like my podcast and webinars, but I also have more in-depth training. I like to provide them with an opportunity to engage with me on a deeper level. This way they constantly feel assured of their investment with me, whether in time or money, and feel it's going to be worthwhile effort reading my emails.

Email 5: Day 11 - Offer (Soft Sell)

Hello, here is some additional content I think you will love... P.S Did you see this offer (insert link)?

Now your sequence kicks into a soft sell approach of offering them content of interest with a "by the way, in case you missed it the first time...". You still want to keep the door open to last-minute action takers because they may not have had time to respond the first time you pitched an offer. A gentle reminder is a good thing and often they will appreciate that you kept in touch. You can send them links to your other books and products to keep the cycle going.

Email 6: Day 14 - Nurture

Now you should continue to nurture your prospects by sending regular and value content on ideally a weekly or monthly basis. If all you can manage is a monthly newsletter that is great. If you have a podcast or write blog posts weekly then share those. Constantly stay in touch so when your next book launch or product comes out, you have engaged fans who are ready to buy. Sometimes people need more time, and sometimes the timing is just not right for them. Don't give up on prospects too soon as you never know when the time is right.

In Summary

So this is really what email marketing is about: testing, trying, tweaking, and filtering. You find something that works, then you rinse and repeat it. It's that simple. It doesn't have to be complicated and literally anyone can do it. Now that you have the system set up, you can let it do its work while you sleep. You can clone this funnel for every book you publish or every project, so you continue the feedback cycle loop. Over time, you would have built a substantial database of engaged and raving fans.

IV

Social Media & Promotions

17

Promotional Ideas

T here are many ways to boost your visibility. Social media, live video, podcasts, webinars, blog posting—they all behave differently. So how do you know what works? You try and test them. Everyone loves getting something for free, especially free books. To get in on the action, all you need to do is invest some time to set it up. Once you get it working, it can start a steady flow of traffic to your website. Free promotion still works as a method as you grow, so as you build your budget, you can reinvest into more targeted paid advertising. This is something I do all the time. I combine free promotions along with paid ads to get the best return.

Publicity and PR

Getting publicity is not as hard as you think. Reporters are always looking for good stories and content. They're busy and if you can make their life easier by providing them with a good story, you raise the odds of being featured. If you can pitch a good idea with a good angle and pre-write the story, you've made it easy for a reporter to simply copy and paste your story. This increases the likelihood that your story is going to be picked up for publication. Remember, you can't pitch the idea that you wrote a book—nobody cares! What is your angle? What is in it for the reader? What story angle is relevant to the readers? What is trending or seasonal that your story speaks to?

There are a few things that you can do to help this process. A publicist's job is to create and nurture relationships with media. You can be your own publicist by reaching out directly. If you know the name of the editor and their direct email address, it's so much more effective than the old school method of sending a mass press release. One of the best ways to find those contacts is to reach out directly to reporters, journalists, and editors through Twitter. I love to trawl through relevant online magazines, blogs, and newspapers. If I find a story that is related to my content, I will find out who wrote the article and I will reach out to them. Many blogs have a call for submissions so it's important to read their guidelines before submitting your pitch.

Publicists love a strong platform that they can leverage. If you already have a social media presence, and links to previous press mentions on your website, it makes it much easier to get more exposure. You want to start the spark by building your platform yourself. Eventually you would have built something of value. Then you will be so busy and so important that you can hire a publicist to do it for you, who can add fire to the flames!

Television & Radio

During my book promotion period for one of my books, I had the opportunity to be interviewed for TV for a local station. It was exciting to experience it, but the results were dismal. The problem was that when the interview went live, the only way people could watch it was if they had access to the cable station. I wasn't even able to see it myself! Unless you were glued to the TV at the particular time it aired, you would have missed it. I had to wait for it to be uploaded to YouTube and by then the traffic to the channel was minimal. Of course, if you get featured on a national TV show like Good Morning America, you will get exposure on a much wider scale. However, the problem I still have with TV and radio is that it doesn't last. Once the episode has aired, it's gone, unless you get access to the replay via YouTube. TV and radio work if you can get the word out *before* your appearance, but the point to media exposure is to attract a new audience, right?

In my opinion, a TV or radio appearance is really about the ego and credibility.

Everyone wants to say they've been featured on TV for street cred. It does help for credibility to show that you had an appearance on TV. If you're good enough for TV, you must be good enough for any kind of interview. This in itself is a win because you can use the video replay of your segment on your website press page to boost your credibility. You can add the media logo to your press page and media kit.

Guest Writing

Writing articles for other websites, blogs, and newspapers is a great way of boosting your visibility and reach. One of the reasons I love written blog posts is that they are evergreen and searchable. Long after your article is featured, you will get the benefit of links to your website, and continual search engine visibility. Google loves good content so if your article is shared or goes viral, you've increased the chances of readers finding you through search in perpetuity.

Many online magazines and blogs offer a submission section on their website so it's important you read their guidelines and rules. Don't just spam an article idea or write something that is not in line with their voice and style. Do your research, read the stories they've featured, and follow the steps to submit your own.

For the majority of these publications you won't get paid, but you're getting free promotion and exposure to a much wider audience which is vital. You might need to write 7 or 10 blog posts before one goes viral so don't expect overnight success. It's definitely an avenue I would add to your arsenal and keep looking out for regular opportunities.

Podcast Interviews

This is one of my favorites, cheapest, and quickest ways of getting publicity online. The beauty of podcasts is that I don't have to leave my home, and I could be sitting in my pj's. I don't have to travel, I don't have to pay to attend an event, and I don't have to be losing time in an airport. Personally, I prefer video, and my podcast "Mimika TV" is video-based for several reasons. My view is that if I'm going to the effort of creating a podcast show, I want to be able to reuse my content on YouTube, Facebook, and iTunes as both audio and video. So yes, you will have to change out your pj's for video, but you're welcome to keep your furry slippers on.

Podcast interviews are not time-based, and they are available to consume freely. This means that long after your interview, people can still find and listen to your content. I love podcast interviews because the links back to my website are invaluable to keeping a flow of web traffic. When somebody searches for you online, your name pops up as a featured guest and it builds your authority. Searchability and search engine optimization are important if you want readers to find you on Google, Amazon, and YouTube since they are search engines.

As a podcast guest, you want to make it easy for the host. Creating a podcast is very time-consuming, and takes a lot of work and financial investment, so show respect and be professional. As a host, one of my pet peeves is when my guests don't bother reading my preparation guides. Their equipment is not set up correctly, they have bad audio and video quality; or they don't show up on time. If you can make it easy for the host, the host will do more to promote you.

Another aspect that drives me nuts is when a guest doesn't bother to share about their interview once it's live. It's not just annoying; it's downright rude! If the host has gone to the trouble and great expense (in time and money) to create a podcast, the least you can do as a guest is re-share the link and graphics. Nothing is free in life, so if you've been given the opportunity to be featured for free, do everyone a favor and help with the promotion. This way everyone wins. Offering great content that serves both your audience and the host's audience is the goal. Perhaps you might get an invite back or referral to other shows, which is always a great thing!

As a podcast host, one of my huge bugbears is when a guest has awful sound. It's too much hard work to edit out echo, scratchy sound, background noise, and low audio levels. It's even worse to try to listen to bad audio. People can forgive blurry video quality, but if the audio is bad, it's like nails on a chalkboard. If you make it hard for listeners, they will simply go elsewhere. And don't get me started about coffee shops! Never, *ever* try to record a podcast in a public place. It's a hellish nightmare to edit and horrible to listen to for the listener with all that background noise.

When doing podcast interviews, at a bare minimum you need a good microphone. Many of the newer Mac computers come with decent built-in microphones, but it can still create an issue with echo (the mic is too close to the speaker). If you're used to using Zoom or Skype for your meetings or client calls, the audio quality is not that important. However, with podcasts a listener's ears are finely tuned to every-little-thing so you need to make the extra effort. If you're serious about pursuing podcasts as an avenue of promotion, make the investment and buy a USB mic. You can get a decent USB mic like the Blue Snowball or the Blue Yeti for under $100.

The same attention to detail applies to video. Senses are tuned in. The viewers are more aware of your mannerisms, what is in the background, and how you speak. This is one of the reasons why I love video because the audience can connect with you much faster when they can actually see you. Most laptops or computers have built in webcams but they're not ideal because you can't control them. With a USB webcam you can use free software to adjust your exposure, color, and focus. Who wants to look like an orange Oompa-Loompa on camera? Pick one that is HD high definition and preferably the latest one on the market if you can afford it (it has all the recent software updated).

Another addition to your kit is a pair of earbuds. The reason for wearing earbuds is to isolate the sound coming through your speakers. You don't want to have an echo or reverb from either you or the host that is picked up by your mic, so by filtering the output into earbuds you get cleaner sound. You don't need anything fancy, just the regular earbuds that come with Apple phones or any brand where you can plug into your computer. You can also get a 2-in-1 headset that has a mic and earphones built in, which may be more affordable to start with.

The last point that I want to highlight when recording an interview, particularly on video using Zoom or Skype, is to ensure that you are on a computer or laptop. Avoid an iPad or your cellphone. Those are fine for simple calls but not for podcasts. Your Internet connection is too unstable and could drop off during the recording. The orientation of the recording matters, too, for video. It does not look good if you're holding your cellphone or iPhone upright, you end up with horrid black boxes to the side of you which screams b-grade when uploaded on YouTube. Think about how you watch TV—it's in a landscape format so you want your podcast recording to look the same.

Preparing for Interviews

- **Equipment**: Be camera-ready, especially for TV and podcast interviews. Investing in equipment like a USB microphone like the (a) Blue Yeti that is a great one, and a (b) HD webcam is needed if you want to be on video and podcasts. Set the Blue Yeti mic to the Cardioid feature (icon with a heart). Grab your earbuds. Download the latest version of Zoom or Skype and keep your software updated. Declutter your background.
- **Wardrobe**: Make sure that you have a professional-looking outfit, your make-up/hair and your talking points ready. In media, things move fast and if you get offered to do a TV appearance, usually it's very last minute. You literally need to be ready at the drop of a hat. I have three go-to outfits (simple, solid colors) that I keep dry cleaned and ready, should the opportunity arise. I have a make-up and travel bag, along with copies of my business card and my One Pager already printed. I have a collection of simple, solid colored shirts that I use for my podcast show and I change them up regularly.
- **Talking points**: Make the headline pop. Just like you are writing an article for a magazine, it needs to grab attention. Ensure that what you share teaches and empowers the audience. You want to whet their appetite so they feel compelled to look you up to find out more. What is it about you that makes you an authority on this topic?
- **Backstory**: To frame the discussion, the host will ask you to share a little bit more about yourself. They don't want a long winded story of every little thing that has happened in your life. Get to the good parts fast. Remember, this is talking-not creative writing-so think about something that is 3

minutes or less. Think about the audience and who will be listening so you can mention parts of your story that are applicable. Think about how elements tie together (e.g. you loved writing as a child in your journal and now you've become a writer). Think of the highlights and the emotion or dramatic moments. Maya Angelou said it best: *"At the end of the day people won't remember what you said or did, they will remember how you made them feel."*

Every time you do an interview, add that link to your press page on your website. If it's a big publication or mention, update your One Pager to reflect that. Don't forget to update your contact information or links if they change. It seems obvious, but this happens all the time when authors create a One Pager or Press Kit then forget about it. Revisit your talking topics as you gain more experience and as you've tested what topics work or not. The other thing to do is to use the logos of the publications on your website for credibility. For example, once I had an article published on the Huffington Post. I created a graphic of their logo and added it to my About page. Immediately, the logo is recognizable and shows credibility.

Giveaways

This is one of my favorite promotional tools to use, especially when you don't have an email list or when you're starting from scratch. When nobody knows you in a certain niche, giveaways can kick-start your email list building. When I pivoted into a new reader market, I combined my efforts with other authors who served the same audience. I knew that their audience is similar to the audience I wanted to target, so bundling my book with theirs was a no-brainer. It was as simple as emailing them and saying, "Hey, I love your book. I'm doing this giveaway and I'd love to buy one for this giveaway that I'm hosting. Would you be able to share about it?"

The one caveat is that you have to pay for the book, unless they graciously offer it as a donation. By showing that you are prepared to pay for their book indicates that you are serious, and not just asking for free stuff. By using the angle that you'd love to promote *them*, you will get their attention. Usually people will say yes because there's nothing they have to do other than send out a tweet or Facebook post. If they're really excited, they might offer to email their audience, and that is like gold! It really does not take a lot of effort, just your willingness to drive it during the giveaway period. You can pay for traffic by running some ads, too, but often just sharing it on your social media platforms gets traction. One thing to remember is you don't want to offer prizes that are too generic. If you offer to give away, for example, a Kindle or Amazon gift card, everyone and their Aunty will enter, only to unsubscribe once it's over. What you want is targeted entrants who like the same books and products similar to yours.

I love using tools like (c) King Sumo or (d) Rafflecopter, and if you're starting out you can use them for free. The beauty is that you can connect it to your email CRM program, so entrants are automatically added to your email funnel.

With giveaways, the trick is to offer a limited time to encourage immediate action. In other words, you offer 10 days to enter and then you do a countdown. Posting reminders at 10 days, 7 days, 3 days, tomorrow's your last day, and lastly today it ends. It creates excitement because one of the requirements for entry is that they post and share online. At the end of the giveaway, you can simply import them into your email program. This of course isn't ideal because they haven't actually opted in and you will probably find a ton of unsubscribes or fake emails. By connecting King Sumo with your email program, it serves two vital purposes. The first is that they immediately get a confirmation email once they enter to confirm they are a legit person and opt into the list. Secondly, once the giveaway ends, you can kick off an email sequence to offer them to buy your book or another offer. This builds your email list and by keeping it clean, you ensure the ones on your list are the right people.

It's important that you make good on your promises and announce a winner. I've seen so many giveaways where there is loads of hype to enter, but I never hear who actually won. This can make people angry because it's false advertising and it's fraudulent. You definitely need to make sure you show the public accountability by announcing the winners and delivering the goods. The software programs like King Sumo and Rafflecopter both offer this function.

Quizzes

Quizzes are a great way to attract and segment cold traffic, especially when you have no list. Where giveaways are for a limited time, quizzes can be offered indefinitely. One of the most successful ways I've seen it used is on a website as the lead generation option. In other words, a new prospect finds your website and the first thing they see is a quiz. By going through the process they are immediately segmenting themselves into buckets that you can organize. Instead of everyone being thrown into a general list bucket, the quiz serves to segment and separate them at the first contact. Once you know exactly who you are speaking to, you can provide more specific and meaningful content. My favorite quiz software is (e) TryInteract or Riddle.

Book Exchanges or Giveaways

Exchanging books and cross promoting with other authors is a great way to grow your email list. If you have a relationship with another author in your genre who has an email list, you can combine efforts. Offer the audience a book exchange: for every book they buy from her, you'll give them a free version of yours or vice versa. Don't underestimate the value and the power in creating relationships with other authors. They're not your competition but your allies. Working with other authors allows you to borrow their audience and is a huge kick-starter when you are starting out. Keep in mind that if you don't have an email list or a large one, you can't approach an author with a huge list. Start off small with authors in the same range who are more keen to push cross promotion so everyone wins.

Amazon Author Central Account

If you are an author, it's imperative you set up an Author Central account. If you already have an Amazon account, you can use the same login or create a new one. Irrespective of your publishing route—traditional or self-published—you need your Author page to connect to your books. As a self-published author, you connect it to your KDP account so you can list your books, run AMS ads, and setup pre-orders. With Amazon, they allow you to list your book for pre-orders for up to 90 days in advance. Listing your book on pre-order is important to help boost your book the day it launches. That is how you get up into the rankings. When Amazon sees a spike of orders, the algorithm kicks in and shows it to more readers. Your author biography and profile photo should be the same as on your website. You can link your social media accounts so they appear as posts on your Author Central page. Every time you write a blog post, it appears on the page. You can create an author account on other platforms, too, where readers frequent like (f) Bookbub and (g) Goodreads to help boost your visibility.

Permafree

Here is a promotional tool that is worth the effort of reading this book. It's a tactic I've used with enormous success that has now become part of my book marketing and list building strategy. It is the concept called the Permafree book. How it works is that you offer the first book in a series, or the first of a certain genre, for free. Yes, you read it right—100% free. Oh, and did I mention free for life? That is what it means: a permafree is a permanently free book. Many authors balk at the idea of giving their work away for free, but it is the single most important thing you can do. Here is why: you are offering a sample or taster of your work. If a reader loves your book, they will want more. It's also a vital part of your email list building strategy. By offering your book for free it gets listed within the free section where it will probably get 10 times more downloads than if you priced it for 99 cents. This works particularly on Amazon. The other aspect is that by continually encouraging free downloads on Amazon, the algorithm sees that your book is popular and continues to promote it along with all your other books. Amazing, right? And you didn't think that being so generous could be so profitable!

One thing to remember is that you have to ask Amazon to price match your book for it to be listed for free. When this same book is listed on other platforms like Barnes and Noble, Kobo or Nook, you can email Amazon customer service to price match. You can use a distribution service like Draft2Digital to upload your books to the other platforms. Once it's listed for free on these sites, then you email Amazon.

Amazon Look Inside Feature

Here is another tip worth gold. In Amazon they provide a "Look Inside" feature. If the reader is curious to see what is inside the book they click the cover and it opens up. It allows you to view a sample of the first 10 or so pages. This is a fabulous way of giving your potential reader a tiny taste of your writing. The reader can assess if the content is of interest without having to purchase the book. The first page they need to see is the free invitation or offer page. The crucial element you need to know is to add this offer page *before* the foreword, book chapters, or content. Many authors and publishers make the mistake of placing the offer page at the end of the book, but that is not where it is effective. Even if your book is offered for free, you are still getting future potential readers and sales just by having that simple page in your book. The beauty is that you don't have to wait for a reader to buy your book to get them on your email list. The offer is available for free to anyone who clicks the "Look Inside" feature.

Think of it just like a landing page on your website. It has a call to action with a link to get an extra bonus like a free gift, download or printable. The important aspect is to direct readers to a specific landing page on your website, not your general website address. For example, this book has its own specific page where you can download the accompanying "Build Your Author Platform with a Purpose Checklist" at www.mimikacooney.com/platform This way I can monitor who joins my email list through this particular book. The one and only thing you can do on this page is click the button to join the list; no links to my blog or other pages. I don't want readers to get confused about what I want them to do.

This strategy has categorically been the single biggest reason I've been able to build my email list so fast. If you only do one thing, use the Look Inside offer page to your advantage and watch your list grow like gangbusters.

Book Promotion Sites

There are a plethora of free book promotion sites available, just Google it and you'll get a list you can pick from. Not every site is going to be related to your content, so you need to do a little bit of digging to find the right ones. It will take a bit of time setting up an account on each one, but it will be worth the effort. Some of the popular ones are (h) Robin Reads, (i) FreeBooksy, (j) Inkitt, (k) E-Reader Girl, (l) Authors Den, etc. Create a profile on book sites like Goodreads and Bookbub to get the most up-to-date information and build your online footprint.

Website Pop Ups

(m) Sumo is an app I use that you install as a plugin on your website. It pops up offers when a reader is browsing your website and works great to grab immediate attention. Although annoying, they work very well. When you connect it to your email program, it builds your email list continually as you drive more targeted traffic to your website.

18

The Power of Video

Video is my jam. I've been into video since the days of VHS tapes and Cindy Lauper hairdos. My interest started in South Africa in 1995 when I took a presenting and on-camera broadcasting class. At the time, I was working at an on-air TV production company and the medium fascinated me. In 2003, I had the opportunity to flex my TV muscles and host a live morning breakfast show in England called "York Today". My days were spent waking up at 5 AM for on-site location shoots, talking ad lib, and throwing together my outfits and hair since we had no budget for a make-up department. It afforded me the opportunity to learn how to interview people to draw out stories that would captivate the audience, and think on my toes.

Naturally with my experience in TV, delving into video was the obvious choice. So in 2013, I launched my first video podcast called "Mimika TV". It was on the cusp of digital video and podcasts before the days of Facebook Live. The only technology that was available at the time was this company that merged the video from Skype, combining my host feed with my guest and streamed it live. I spent $350 *per* episode for the luxury of this service, and after 5 episodes, called it quits because it was too expensive. Despite the costs, I firmly believed that video was going to change the online competitive landscape. I guess I was right!

Video has evolved over the years. We've ditched the hairspray and VHS tapes for the power of Facebook Live, YouTube, and Insta Stories. All this technology within the palm of our hand and for free! Video is so effective because it's the best way to get to know someone and trust them. They can see your body language, your eye contact and hear your voice. Video is the next best thing to meeting someone in person.

Today, with the likes of Facebook Live, you can easily dip your toe into the medium to test it out. You don't need fancy equipment or have to pay for subscriptions. The beauty is that Facebook favors video over all other content—above text or photo posts. The good news is that once you get the attention of the algorithm by posting videos, it starts to recognize that you're posting videos, and it starts to show your content to more people. Just like with Amazon, the more valuable content you share, the more your valuable content gets shared. As of this writing, all this is offered for free, so I would suggest you get on the video bandwagon fast before Facebook changes their mind and starts charging.

The best news is that you can start using your cellphone. You can easily just hop onto Facebook, speak to the audience, make eye contact, and get feedback. Even if you don't get a lot of live viewers, the replay will get even more views. Its shareability is what is so effective because with a click of a button, you can spread your ideas and reach a wider audience. I firmly believe in repurposing your content. Whether you create it as a Facebook video, or an Instagram video, you can reuse it by uploading it to other platforms like YouTube (and vice versa).

Tips for Video

1. You need to have a **strong Internet connection,** especially when you are streaming live. In an ideal world, you want to plug directly into an ethernet cable and you can with a laptop or computer. I advise this for my guests when we record video podcast interviews to ensure a more stable connection through Zoom. However, not everyone has access to an ethernet cable and so may have to rely on Wifi (especially using a cellphone). In this case, it's imperative you shut down any other device that may use the bandwidth like Netflix or YouTube. No uploading or

downloading content during the recording, either. You don't want your video to stutter, freeze, or hang.

2. **Good lighting** to light up the eyes is important to establish eye contact. You don't want your eyes looking like black dots or have shadows. Besides it looking creepy, it comes across as untrustworthy. If you're standing in front of a window and the window is behind you, you're going to be backlit. The window is going to be brighter so your camera will make you appear like a dark silhouette. A simple fix is to turn around and have your face towards where the light is so you are well lit. Whether you use a big window for natural light or whether you have video lights, always have the lights facing you. A good point of reference is if you can see the color of your eyes, then you are well lit. If you are outside, avoid direct sunlight so you don't squint. Instead, stand under a tree in its shadow for even lighting.

3. Your **position on camera** makes a difference, too. Make sure you sit up straight with your head positioned along the rule of thirds. A great way of knowing if you are centered correctly is having your eyes in the top third of the screen. You want to have a bit of wiggle room at the top of your head, and you don't want to cut off the top of your head. You also don't want to be too small or too low in the frame, or it looks like your sinking out of frame. A good habit is to have your head and shoulders within view with enough room below your shoulders for lower third graphics or your name. You also don't want to be so far away that you look like you're floating in the middle of space. So a good rule of thumb is to use a selfie stick and test how big your head would be in the frame.

4. With Facebook and with Instagram, you can use upright video, but I personally prefer to record video in **landscape format**. I want to be able to reuse my videos on YouTube and avoid those black boxes that appear on the sides when using a portrait orientation. The simple fix is to hold your camera or cell phone sideways, or use a selfie stick or tripod.

5. If you do a Facebook live video, you do have the option to **download the video file** so you can re-upload it to other platforms like YouTube. If you record a video offline, you can add it to your YouTube channel without

any issues. However, if you want to share a video on Facebook, you are better off uploading it directly to Facebook because Facebook doesn't like links to YouTube. In fact, I've found any direct links to YouTube are heavily penalized and the reach tanks. Remember, each platform is designed to keep you there so there is no incentive for Facebook to promote YouTube or vice versa. So my advice is to download the video file, re-upload it directly to your YouTube channel and copy the code to your website blog. It's what we call the embed code which makes it easy for you to share a YouTube or Facebook video within another page.

6. You need to pick your **talking topics** before hitting record. With live video, there is no script needed, but you do want to have an idea in mind of what you want to talk about. Viewers want to know what they can expect. Starting with an introduction or teaser of what you will be covering is a great way of grabbing their attention and keeping them watching. Another thing I would avoid doing when starting a live video is telling the audience you're waiting for other people to join and then do radio silent. This is live, people; don't keep people hanging! Besides, you need to remember that the replay will get much more views than when it's live, so why would they stick around to watch if you've made them wait? Just start the video and get right to the talking points as soon as possible or you will lose the audience. With live, it's good practice to acknowledge viewers by name but don't make it a chat fest (unless that is your goal). Say hello, introduce the topic of discussion, greet a few of the names and get back to talking. Throughout the video, you can come back to your live audience and answer questions, but keep the conversation flowing.

7. Make it a habit to ask your **audience to take action**. Whether it is commenting, visiting your website, signing up to your email list, or buying your offer, give them something to do. Asking for interaction is crucial to getting engagement because the more comments, likes, and shares you can get, the more visibility the video will get. Ending with a call to action like "grab my free book or download" is a fabulous way of wrapping up and giving the audience a way of getting on your email list.

8. If you want to go a step further, you can **transcribe** your video and use the text for a blog post or content for a book. With one video, you've now created content for 3 platforms and sped up your workflow. By thinking smart and preparing in advance, you can crank out content very easily.

Virtual Summits

I love being part of summit interviews with other experts. Adding your expertise to a group of other authors or speakers who have knowledge on a certain topic enables you to be positioned as an expert in your market. A summit is a series of trainings focused on a particular topic. They are limited to a specific time frame. They can be hosted live and in-person, but the most popular format is hosting it online. Virtual video summits are the most popular. I much prefer the online version because all you have to do is record it in the comfort of your home, then the host does the rest of the heavy lifting with the editing. Just like with podcast interviews, as a guest your only commitment is being available to record the interview and helping with the promotion. Virtual Summits are a perfect way to build your email list, especially when you're starting out. The very first summit I was a part of brought in over 300 email signups in one day and fast tracked my list building efforts.

Summit interviews work best when they have limited availability that drives traffic and views within a short time period (anything from 5-30 days). The standard practice is to offer it to the public to watch live for free on the day, then offer the replay recordings as a paid option. This works great if viewers don't have the time to watch live, and like to work through the content in their own time. For the guest experts, it works great because they get an affiliate commission for the viewers they bring in (usually 50%). It also works great for the host to recoup the costs involved with producing the summit. Every summit host runs it differently and it all depends on the overall goal: to make money or for list building, or both.

The summit host will require that you share, post, and email your audience to get them signed up. I've seen summits hosted over 7 to 10 days, and some over 30 days, but that's overkill. Think about the audience, how much time do they realistically have to listen to or watch videos? My school of thought is to make it shorter for better engagement to avoid audience fatigue.

In 2018, I hosted my own Purpose Power Summit over 7 days. It centered around the subject of purpose and focused on women who are interested in finding God's purpose for their life. This worked great to help build my audience in a new genre before I published my book. My goal was to build my email list, so I decided to make it available for free without charging for replays to widen my reach. As the host, it took a lot of effort and time. Tasks included reaching out to guests, scheduling interviews, recording the interviews, editing the interviews, promotion setup, creating graphics, setting up the email funnel, setting up a giveaway, and driving engagement during the summit period. It is no small feat, especially if you are technologically challenged, and requires a commitment of 3 to 6 months to prepare for a professional end result.

How I was able to keep the excitement high during the summit was to offer giveaways and prizes. It's important to get people sharing and talking about it, so making it easy for your guests to share is vital. Create graphics, copy and paste text, easily share links and a guideline of what you need them to do and when. The success of a summit depends on creating relationships with the right experts, producing a professional end product, setting it up correctly, and pushing promotion.

Webinars

Whenever I want to test a new book idea or training, I will host a free webinar. Before I go to the effort of creating a course or writing a book, I like to test the audience first. This way, if my idea sucks, all I've lost is some time. Webinars work great for list building and for driving sales. Most of the time, a webinar is designed to titillate the audience by sharing a small part of the overall training, and offering an opportunity to buy a larger product to learn more. For coaches, consultants, and authors, this works great to drive sales to your latest endeavour as you can measure its success immediately by the number of takers you get. My favorite software to start with is (n) WebinarJam and if you have a bigger budget, you can use (o) GoToWebinar.

19

Paid Advertising

Paying for advertising, even for a free book, is still a good use of time and money. You are attracting a highly targeted audience, where you can drill down to know their interests and demographics. You can be very specific, especially using Facebook and its ability to segment an audience down to a zip code. Amazon advertising is growing fast and is offering some incredible results when it comes to keeping a book selling long past its launch date.

Facebook Ads

Facebook advertising changes as often as the tides, so you will need to keep up with their latest developments. What doesn't change is the effectiveness of targeting a very specific market for great results. Gone are the days of posting online for free and getting immediate results. Love it or hate it, Facebook is a business aimed at making money. The good news, though, is that they want to encourage advertisers to use their ads platform so it is in their interests to help you get results. Facebook ads drive very targeted traffic and that is why they work so well.

One thing I must mention here is you set up Facebook ads through your business page; don't confuse it with your personal profile. Your personal profile page is just about you, usually using your actual name. According to their rules, you shouldn't post any business-related stuff on your personal profile. However, you're more than welcome to share your business page posts to your personal page.

Borrowing somebody else's audience is a great way to start attracting an audience who likes similar things. If you like a certain person's page that is similar to mine, you might like what I have to offer. Facebook ads don't have to be super expensive to start with, but you can blow through your budget very quickly if you don't know what you're doing.

You can start with a small daily budget of $5 a day and test it. The Facebook ad algorithm usually takes up to 2 weeks to recognize the kind of audience you're targeting, so you may need to set up a test ad to get it started. Facebook loves video, and engagement on video posts are at least twice as effective as plain text or still photos. The great news is that you can hop on Facebook Live, do a video, and then pay to promote it using an ad or pay to boost the post. The more people who see, like, comment, and share your content from your page, the more people Facebook will show it to. The point is engagement and action, and the best way to monitor this is through email signups. Personally, I prefer to pay for ads that drive viewers to a landing page on my website, a blog post, or a webinar signup page. That way, I'm not guessing who took action, I can tell immediately by the number of email signups I get. It all comes down to your goals, what you want to achieve, and measuring results so you don't burn through cash on a windy day.

Amazon Ads

Amazon ads are a very affordable way for you to drive targeted traffic to books long after their launch date. Amazon is the biggest seller of books, so it makes sense to be where your readers are actively searching for their next find. With social media, people are in a passive state of mind randomly scrolling. With Amazon, people are actively searching for something to buy and are ready to part with their cash, so it's a much easier sell. You can target readers using either keywords or targeting books that are similar to yours.

I've been testing Amazon ads for over a year and have seen a steady increase in sales in my books, the more targeted and focused I've become. As a matter of fact, my book, *Worrier to Warrior*, is selling better now, 18 months later, than it did during launch month. By using Amazon ads, I've been able to create a steady, monthly flow of orders and new fans.

One thing to remember with the ads is that you want them to test and monitor results. It's not something you set up and forget; you need to keep your finger on the pulse and continually tweak your ad sets. However, don't let it scare you because once you get the hang of it, they'll become a great arsenal in your platform building toolkit.

Need more help?

If running ads is foreign or scares you, don't worry; I can help. If you would like to learn more about leveraging paid advertising to sell more books, and the steps to self publishing your book for bestseller success, check out my training **Self Publishing Mastermind** www.selfpublishingmastermind.com

Extra Offers

Complimentary Checklist

Download the FREE printable Platform Building Checklist:
www.mimikacooney.com/platform

More Books

If you enjoyed this book, check out other books in my collection:
Mindset Make Over www.mimikacooney.com/mindset
Worrier to Warrior www.mimikacooney.com/warrior
Angus The Goat www.angusthegoat.com

More Free Resources

For a list of my other resources visit my website:
https://www.mimikacooney.com

Platform Purpose Membership Community

If you'd like to join a membership community of Faith-based writers, speakers, and entrepreneurs who are building their platform and leveraging online marketing, come join **Platform Purpose** and become a member today:
https://www.platformpurpose.com

Self Publishing Mastermind

If you would like to learn more about leveraging paid advertising to sell more books, and the steps to self publishing your book for bestseller success, check out my training **Self Publishing Mastermind**: www.selfpublishingmaster-mind.com

Reviews

Your opinions are important and I truly value your feedback. As an author it is important to get **Reviews** from valuable readers like you so that future readers can make better decisions. Please help me by leaving your honest review on your preferred bookstore or platform. Thank you!

Share

If you enjoyed this book and found the content useful, please share it with your friends online. Use the hashtag #PlatformwithaPurpose and tag me @mimikacooney so I can thank you:)

Free Store Discount

Would you like royalty free stock photos for social media, ebooks, wall art, screensavers, T-shirts and merchandise? Use this coupon to get **$5 FREE** to spend in my shop at:
   https://www.shopmimika.com
   COUPON CODE: **PPBOOKOFFER**

About the Author

Mimika Cooney is a Best Selling Author, Podcast host of "Mimika TV", Entrepreneur, and Award Winning Photographer. Huffington Post nominated Mimika as one of "50 Women Entrepreneurs to Follow in 2017".

Mimika has published books in the Business/Marketing, and Christian Living genres. Her book "Mindset Make-Over: How to Renew your Mind and Walk in God's Authority" remained in the top 5 positions on Amazon for 12 months since publication. The book "Worrier to Warrior: A Mother's Journey from Fear to Faith" launched as an Amazon #1 Best Seller.

Mimika is the founder of Platform Purpose, a membership for thought leaders, authors, speakers, ministers and entrepreneurs who want to learn how to leverage marketing, branding, media, publicity, writing and self publishing. She is also the creator of the course Self Publishing Mastermind that helps smart writers self-publish using a system.

Mimika is passionate about empowering and equipping individuals to fulfill their God-given purpose, position their value, spread their message and make an impact in the marketplace. Mimika loves to spark honest conversations, blaze a trail where others fear to tread, and infuse positivity wherever she goes. She is known for building community, creating connections and helping others share their story with passion and purpose.

Mimika is a native of South Africa and citizen of the USA. She is a ferocious reader, enjoys watching soppy romcoms and cuddling on the sofa with her 3 kids and dashing husband of 23 years. When she is not dreaming up creative concepts, writing books or hosting her podcast; she will be found perfecting her spins on the ice as a competitive adult figure skater.

For more resources visit:
Mimika's Website https://www.mimikacooney.com
Platform Purpose https://platformpurpose.com
Self Publishing Mastermind https://selfpublishingmastermind.com

Connect with Mimika online:
Facebook https://www.facebook.com/themimikacooney
Instagram https://www.instagram.com/mimikacooney
YouTube https://youtube.com/c/mimikacooney
Twitter https://twitter.com/mimikacooney
Pinterest https://www.pinterest.com/mimikacooney

Books by Mimika Cooney:
Worrier to Warrior: A Mother's Journey from Fear to Faith
Mindset Make-Over: How to Renew your Mind and Walk in God's Authority
Build Your Author Platform with a Purpose: Marketing Strategies for Writers

References

Part 1: Platform Building

Chapter 1 - Introduction

Chapter 2 - Why Build a Platform?

(a) Mindset Make Over: How to Renew your Mind and Walk in God's Authority:
https://www.mimikacooney.com/platformlinks

Chapter 3 - What Is a Platform?

(b) Jerry Jenkins https://jerrysguild.com

(c) The term "Platform" https://www.dictionary.com/browse/platform?s=t
(accessed 8/25/2019)

Chapter 4 - Avoid Wasting Time, Money & Effort
  (d) Reedsy https://reedsy.com/r/mimika-cooney
  (e) Fiverr https://www.fiverr.com
  (f) 99designs https://99designs.com
  (g) Upwork https://www.upwork.com

Chapter 5 - Establishing Authority as an Influencer
  (h) Joshua Bell Experiment https://wapo.st/2lUHkX4 (accessed 8/25/2019)

Chapter 6 - Analogue Days

Chapter 7 - What Publishers & Readers Want

(i) Rachelle Gardner https://rachellegardner.com/the-dreaded-author-platform (accessed 8/25/2019)

(j) Survey https://www.surveymonkey.com/results/SM-MX3ZCQYY (accessed 8/25/2019)

(k) Marie Force https://blog.marieforce.com/survey-indicates-indie-publishing-is-pot-of-gold-for-some-work-in-progress-for-many (accessed 8/25/2019)

(l) Self Publishing Mastermind https://www.selfpublishingmastermind

Chapter 8 - Write the Right Book

(m) Draft2Digital https://www.draft2digital.com/r/Y3ErAq

(n) BookBaby http://www.bookbaby.com

(o) Lulu Press https://www.lulu.com

(p) Ingram Spark https://ingramspark.com

(q) Amazon KDP kdp.amazon. com

(r) Reedsy Professional Editor/ Proofreader https://reedsy.com/r/mimika-cooney

(s) Book Cover Designers https://thebookcoverdesigner.com/designers/book-covers-art

(t) Creative Market https://creativemarket.com/?u=mimika

(u) Self Pub Book Covers https://selfpubbookcovers.com

(v) Author Platform https://platformpurpose.com

Part 2: Branding Blueprint

Chapter 9 - Branding Blueprint

(a) Simon Sinek *Start with Why* https://simonsinek.com/product/start-with-why

(b) Sally Hogshead *Fascinate: Your 7 Triggers to Persuasion and Captivation* https://www.howtofascinate.com/store/books

Chapter 10 - Understanding Your Marketing Strategy

Chapter 11 - Personalized Website
   (c) Jerry B. Jenkins Writers Guild https://jerrysguild.com
   (d) Serious Writer https://www.seriouswriter.com
   (e) Hope Writers https://www.hopewriters.com
   (f) Masterclass https://www.masterclass.com

Part 3: Email Marketing

Chapter 12 - Build an Email List of Raving Fans

Chapter 13 - Create a Freebie Offer That Hooks Readers Fast

Chapter 14 - Landing Pages
   (a) Optimize Press https://www.optimizepress.com

Chapter 15 - Email Funnels that Sell while You Sleep

Chapter 16 - How to Set Up a CRM
   (a) Active Campaign http://bit.ly/2uLrEXl
   (b) MailChimp http://bit.ly/2lXPUEv
   (c) Mailer Lite http://bit.ly/2knL570
   (d) Drip https://www.drip.com
   (e) Constant Contact http://bit.ly/2mikQPT
   (f) Aweber https://www.aweber.com
   (g) Get Response https://www.getresponse.com
   (h) Mad Mimi https://madmimi.com

Part 4: Social Media & Promotions

Chapter 17 - Promotional Ideas

    (a) Blue Yeti https://www.bluedesigns.com/products/yeti

    (b) HD webcam https://www.logitech.com/en-us/video/webcams

    (c) King Sumo https://kingsumo.com

    (d) Rafflecopter https://www.rafflecopter.com

    (e) TryInteract https://interact.grsm.io/mimikacooney8852

    (f) Bookbub https://www.bookbub.com/profile/mimika-cooney

    (g) Goodreads https://www.goodreads.com/author/show/5321403.Mimika_Cooney

    (h) Robin Reads https://robinreads.com

    (i) FreeBooksy https://www.freebooksy.com

    (j) Inkitt https://www.inkitt.com

    (k) E-Reader Girl https://ereadergirl.com

    (l) Authors Den http://www.authorsden.com

    (m) Sumo https://sumo.com

Chapter 18 - The Power of Video

    (n) WebinarJam https://www.webinarjam.com

    (o) GoToWebinar https://www.gotomeeting.com/webinar

Chapter 19 - Paid Advertising

Disclaimer: some links are affiliate links and earn me a small commission on each sale.

Notes

CPSIA information can be obtained
at www.ICGtesting.com
Printed in the USA
LVHW011030041119
636239LV00013B/1729

9 781732 284869